AF651463

Concept Publishing Co.
Rs 250/-

CONFLICTS AND CO-EXISTENCE – INDIA

By the same author

Science and Technology in India's Transformation (Concept, 1986)
Development of the Resources of the Sea INDIA (Concept, 1989)

CONFLICTS AND CO-EXISTENCE INDIA

J.N. NANDA

CONCEPT PUBLISHING COMPANY, NEW DELHI 110059

ISBN 81-7022-302-4

First Published 1991

© Jatinder Nath Nanda (*b.* 1920)

Published and Printed by
Ashok Kumar Mittal
Concept Publishing Company
A/15-16, Commercial Block, Mohan Garden
NEW DELHI 110059 (India)

Lasertypeset by
Microtech Advance Printing Systems (Pvt.) Ltd.
H-13, Bali Nagar
NEW DELHI 110015

DEDICATED TO CHILDREN
AND
A FUTURE OF
LOVE AND TRUST

CONTENTS

PREFACE

COMMUNAL TENSIONS and passions can be witnessed in all their ugliness only during actual riots or attacks of terrorists. This book does not deal with any individual riots or incidents. We wish only to ponder over the mental make-up which is responsible and our indifference to the growth of feelings of estrangement deep down, in spite of strenuous efforts throughout the ages by so many pious people in spreading the gospel of charity, love and forgiveness. How people can become self-centred and bigoted and even neighbours and brothers can become victims of hatred and distrust?

Suddenly a man rushes to the driver of a bus and forces him to stop the bus at a relatively secluded spot. Few others brandishing arms separate out members of the marked minority community and gun them to death. Similar terrorism stalks the 'outsider' villagers in the tribal Bodo lands. Such incidents do produce tales of heroism from either group when certain brave and true individuals stand up to the lunatic killers. In time, national monuments will be erected at such massacre spots. A respected family in an affluent sector of our capital city is forced into hiding in a number of houses of their neighbours because an irate mob is after their blood in revenge of the crimes allegedly committed by some other members of the same community. A selection committee is convinced that a Mr. X happens to be most suitable, but it is compelled by the framers of selection rules to select Mr. Y since he is of the preferred community, sex or linguistic group. Such happenings lead eventually to the isolation of various groups and the fragmented nation fails to progress. For peaceful progress within the country we must deliberately foster the feeling of mutual acceptance, co-existence and love. In India the simplest device would be to encourage common worship and common recreation. Thus, local festivals, local deities, common objects of adoration like the trees, stones, relics and tombs become important and are not to be dismissed lightly.

Though a cultural unit for ages, India has emerged as a political entity only after being united in bondage in the British empire. This political entity has yet to grow into an integrated nation. One could dismiss the partition of India as a birth pang, but it will not be in the national interest to passively accept the recurring conflicts in different places, simply as growing pains. It is necessary for all interested in the progress of a united India to understand the nature of conflicts, in general, and the conflicts actually occurring in the country in particular. We wish to develop democratically assuring fundamental rights and economic equality to all. Such a realization must reach all, only then can conflicts be prevented or resolved to the greater strength and happiness of all.

In this small book, we shall be dealing with communal conflicts, regional and language problems besides inter-State and Centre-State relations. We will not be concerned with peculiar minority groups like lepers, beggars, etc. The major consideration for internal peace is a better grasp of secularism and of the scientific approach. Religion brings man closer to man and can be a guide for social and cultural life of all Indians. The communal conflicts are the result of a narrow outlook and double morality of the fanatics in any religion.

For any progress, international peace, sense of national security and rule of law are required. India's policy of peaceful co-existence and friendship with all as well as mutual co-operation in areas of common interest is examined. The policies of secularism and peaceful co-existence are almost natural to the Hindu view of life. I have put forward some suggestions for encouraging humanism among Indians of all faiths and creeds.

I am indebted to many friends, especially Prof. D.S. Kothari and Dr. A.R. Kidwai, for valuable encouragement. I hope this work will be appreciated by them and others anxious for a bright future of India – a future of peace, progress and goodwill.

I would like to conclude with, a couple of Mahatma Gandhi's apt quotations:

> "Intolerance betrays want of faith in one's cause." "The golden rule of conduct is mutual toleration, seeing that we will never all think alike."

J.N. NANDA

1

CONFLICTS AND NATIONAL AWAKENING

Introduction

WHERE NATIONS can flounder through internal or external conflicts, they can also grow in strength and stature when there is resolution of conflicts. Without conflicts as well as with inadequate conflict management, nations may degenerate and become incapable of meeting the demands of changing times. In this book we are mostly concerned with national awakening and technological modernization in India. The situation in the late 1980s is of gloom tinged with optimism for the next century. The worries have arisen due to an upsurge of narrow caste and traditional interests overlapping impatience of the downtrodden. These happenings are partly the growing pains of the nation and beyond the current conflicts lie strength and vitality.

Nations are born in conflict and in peace they progress. Most nations have been born through victorious struggles. The USA, China, Vietnam, Yugoslavia, India, Indonesia are relatively recent examples.

In the final analysis a nation exists in the minds of its people. India was a nation even before its independence in 1947 and South Africa with its overwhelming black population is already a nation awaiting the victorious conclusion to the struggle there, and so is Palestine of the PLO. When the people have a feeling of kinship for each other and believe in a bright future through unity, nationalism overcomes all odds. When important groups rightly or wrongly wish to pull in divergent ways, the nation will survive, and flourish only when the rebellious minority is convinced of its future well-being better through national unity. Such situations exist in Cyprus and Sri Lanka at present.

The minorities have always existed in all states and the national minorities have formed a number of new independent States in Europe in recent times, some of which had later agreed to become autonomous parts of bigger federations or unions. Often a new State founded by an erstwhile minority is beset by its own minority problems, e.g. Pakistan which had to break with the independence of its Bangla part though not strictly, its minority part. The present Pakistan also has its minorities though it prides itself as an Islamic State of pure nationals. It has now its Sindhi-speaking and Pashto-speaking minorities poised on carving autonomous States.

Indian nationalism could, during its struggle for freedom, overcome communal pulls and gave India a workable constitution. However, the communalism and regionalism have lately shown new resurgence. For India to emerge stronger from the present conflicts the struggle to win people's minds is now going on. We shall try to analyze the factors that stoke the fires of disaffection and steps that could be taken to underscore unity in our diversity.

Nationalism

The rights, freedom and modern amenities for purposeful life can be achieved with dignity only by a people who are free and master of their resources, plans and policies in the international community of nations. Development will be retarded and resources frittered away if there is dissent and sizable groups agitate against common rules and procedures set up by the nation constitutionally. The citizens of a nation must feel kinship, co-operate and be helpful.

A nation lives in a national State with boundaries recognized as such by the world and is supposed to have well-recognized individuality often of one or more of the following: language, culture, customs, values, distinctive arts and literature, music and dance, etc. Nations like to buttress their individuality with a constitution, flag, motto, national anthem, bird, poet, etc. Religious ideas are important in moulding social interactions and have a force of their own. No one can modernize a nation from outside. Where the national citizens are in a position to benefit, they will do so from other's example or advice. A country must be free to develop according to its own genius. This is why most colonies soon give up their tutelage to the mother country. Nationalism has proven greater than conquering empires. A nation of different nationalities is an admission of failure as a single nation. Such a pseudonation will have its political parties split into ethnic or religious branches; the non-congress parties in India are attempting to federate into such a political party.

The national State as we recognize it now came into being in Europe in the 18th and 19th centuries, after the break up of the Spanish, French, Swedish and Turkish empires. A world of nations ensued after the break up of the British, French and other empires after the two World Wars. Nations have evolved through conflicts. When a viable group feels hemmed in by distant authority and struggles with success to be free from it, a new nation emerges overcoming any internal centrifugal forces on account of minority sensitiveness. After a few years' experience, there will always be, within the geographical region of the new nation, some minority not fully satisfied with the set-up. This can lead to internal disturbance or even a civil war. Minority problems will arise irrespective of the size of a nation and have to be met skilfully in mutual interest. The USA, Spain, Russia and many nations of Africa had civil wars. The minority issue has loomed large in Ireland, Somalia, China, Pakistan, Sri Lanka, etc. Modernization will be speeded up if the resources and manpower in a country are sizable. The key to modernization is the skill and capability of the leadership and the population of the country. These qualities have helped certain small nations like South Korea, Taipei, Hong Kong, Singapore, Denmark, Sweden, Switzerland, etc., to develop. Partly this must also be due to the political environment which has been fully utilized by them. To compensate for some coolness in the East-West relationship, the Third World countries have invented the concepts of non-alignment, south-south co-operation, treaties of friendship, self-help and financial and political support to various organs of the United Nations. A nation has to be aware of its special endowment and skills to plan its progress, e.g. modern Spain has developed tourist industry, Iceland its fishing industry and Arab and West Asian lands their oil wealth.

Decentralization

Nations arise because there were successful revolts against the central authority of an empire or a large country. Thus, for a country to hold together there should be enough central authority. So that the central authority is not frittered away in needless conflict and controversy, the central authority itself must decentralize some of its powers and create dispersed centres for meeting local challenges and monitoring the development plans and needs of the diverse population and diverse ecologies. A nation will last only if the national writ is upheld by free choice and the central authority is strong enough to quell violent dissent and thwart any interference or threats from outside. The primary concern of a nation, like that of a living organism, is security which in part depends on the size including physical resources, the wealth and industrialization, etc. Even a most retiring and recluse nation can suffer aggression. For aggression, genuine fault of the weaker nation is not necessary. The existence of a nation means acceptance by the people concerned of a central authority and they being against fragmentation of that authority. Decentralization of the execution of planned progress is necessitated by the human requirements of freedom in decision-making, since human beings do not function as robots. Decentralization harnesses the distributed talent in every nook and corner of the country for better physical, cultural and intellectual life.

The Soviet perestroika is a recognition of this fact. Decentralization does not mean development in isolated pockets, the district level or unit level planning must make allowances for repercussions and dependence on other units while reasonable co-operation would be guaranteed by the whole national organization. Systematic concepts properly applied will avoid unnecessary duplication, inefficiency and uneconomical efforts For insurance against any national crisis, the differences in language, caste, creed or of domicile must be kept in low key allowing more play to the theme of unity in diversity. In certain large federating countries, law and order authority is decentralized to even district and sometimes institutional levels, but a distinction is made for federal offences. For the supremacy of federal needs a federal investigating agency and police is established which can demand co-operation from local enforcement agencies. It was this kind of provision which enabled the U.S. Supreme Court to force State discriminatory laws and practices into retreat before the civil rights law came into force in 1964.

In India lack of central law enforcement agencies sometimes permits atrocities on Scheduled Castes/Scheduled Tribes to go unpunished when existing laws are flouted through a nexus between local politicians, contractors and exploiting elements. No one can deny that a real need for the devolution of more privileges existed for the backward classes and tribes and the less-developed areas, but this cannot be at the cost of the basic concepts of national citizenship. Even countries, like Canada and Australia allow some immigration by foreign nationals depending on the skills and resources being in short supply from their own nationals. The banning of all immigration to certain States and territories from other parts of the country is an invitation to disintegration of the nation. Certain desirable immigration from other States of India must have an admission quota each year especially when there is full freedom to citizens of the restrictive territories to move out and settle anywhere in the country and they are using this privilege more and more. Outsiders depending on their know-how and capital should be welcomed for settling in the backward areas. They should be permitted to strike roots and have stake in permanent development. We must not go back to the anarchic decentralization of India of despotic princelings who would only think of development of themselves and their palaces.

Decentralized planning, so essential for freeing initiative and creativity from bureaucratic long-distance lethargic inputs, cannot ignore systematic approach to development and dovetailing of resources with other parts of the country. Some of the essential raw materials, energy production, etc., may have to be bartered with others for own requirements of preferred inputs. Decentralization is necessary, therefore, for more local enterprise and creativity, for determining local priorities and for promotion of local culture, arts, tourism, etc.

Centralization must have overriding attention in many ways. If any particular local procedure is found repugnant to the strengthening of the national identity, federal enforcement of correction must be carried out. In no part of India, for example, no one can show disrespect to national symbols like the national flag, the national anthem or the national Constitution under whatever pretext. Teaching of history and philosophy must be rid of the bias of writers against the interests of the nation. There is no need for imposition of uniformity or so-called Indianization on the people. A nation will have to be the sum of its parts and no part can be allowed to make a negative contribution to the sum.

Modernization

It stands for a country being prepared for receiving benefits of achievements in science, technology, communications, medicine, management, etc. Modernization in Europe began with the Industrial

Revolution. While feudal or military regimes restricted modernization to the governing classes only, countries having more broad-based governments, like the Western democracies, progressed rapidly. Russian modernization picked up speed with the electrification after the Russian Revolution of 1917. They have had another silent revolution of fresh structuring and openness in 1985 for further rapid advancement. Colonial governments naturally restricted modernization to the extent it could help exploit further the colony. Any advances that could loosen their grip was frowned upon. Modernization of India began haltingly with the spread of railway communication. India, however, would have continued to remain primitive in industry but for the necessities imposed by the two world wars. Planned development and modernization really started after independence in 1947. Restoration and renewal of India's handicrafts and native skills for beauty and art as well as for exports are also elements in its modernization. Modern designs, tailored materials and engineered simple human-powered machines have been grafted on to handicraft skills. Modernization does not infringe on ethnic distinctiveness if certain dress or style is cherished. Assimilation evolves with time. An able leadership following Gandhi and Nehru placed India on the proper path of progress through democratic socialistic pattern and secularism so essential for a large underdeveloped country. In the absence of private skills and risk capital, central planning and public sector were given leading roles. As skills and financial resources increased, more and more decentralization in planning and decision-making is being encouraged for harnessing distributed initiative and talents. Planned progress is necessary in the interest of better living standards for all Indians in whichever State or territory of India they may be residing. This required a broad vision and awareness of conditions in other countries. Looking only to the selfish gains of one's class and one's neighbourhood will not benefit everyone. For any modernization of agriculture, which is the backbone of Indian production, modern machines, newly developed seeds, protection against plant diseases and destructive insects are required. There is requirement of agricultural research and training institutions, fertilizer factories, a flourishing chemical and mechanical industry, readiness for large inputs of irrigation water and power, besides co-operative marketing of inputs and produce. This requires large regional planning. The same can be said about planning of material and energy resources. Conflicts slow down progress and modernization. Better management practice is necessary to handle and keep contented efficient labour. Free discussion is the best guarantee for development of the understanding of the common man for the goals and the means and the national policies. Development implies creation of new capabilities in people for meeting new aspirations. Ethnic individuality need not hamper the planned progress and progress must harness any special talents encouraged by ethnicity.

The vested interest and the exploiting classes are not for modernization involving literacy, information and awakening of the common man. They will make common cause with obscurantism or propagate short-cuts like the expropriation of the wealth and rights of the weaker sections by the elect. As the modernization progressed, the caste rights, or rather the denial of rights to the outcastes, have been the first casualty. Modernization does not countenance the exploitation of the backward classes or the impoverishment of the eco-system by the marauding contractors. Modernization cannot suit those who are interested in keeping the common man chained in ignorance, superstition and subservience. The misguiding slogans are then raised about outsiders taking up development jobs and managing their wealth of land, water, forests, minerals, etc. Even fault is found with the daily-wage labourers migrating seasonally to the work areas before going back to their homes. Their fault is that they speak a different language or worship different gods. The symbol of modernization is modern communications but the opposition damages the buses and trains. This is then an additional setback to the development plans. The apparently irrational vandalism is actually a set pattern since the agitation actually is against development, other pretexts are only incidental to spark the agitation. The salvation of our people, however, lies in mutual co-operation and husbanding the available resources with 'outside' assistance, if necessary, so long as they themselves control the planned progress. The Universal Declaration of Human Rights, adopted by the United Nations in 1946, declares: 'All human beings are born free and equal in dignity and rights.' They are endowed with reason and conscience and should act towards one another in a spirit of brotherhood.

Internationalism

Internationalism has grown in importance due to the realization of interdependence of people of the world. We are mainly concerned with the conflicts within India, but naturally India's relations with other nations will receive some attention. The conflicts, however, still rage over the world stage. There is hope due to the establishment and continued working of the United Nations in a limited way. The current wave in support of regional groupings at various levels of functioning is sure to consolidate peace and lead to the resolution of many conflicts. The good offices of the Secretary General are being used more and more for international rapprochement between estranged nations. There are many international agencies engaged in co-operative services and international development aid and transfer of technology. International law is also crystallizing through consensus. Indian posture in favour of internationalism is well established. India had been helping reconstruction work in Burma through their non-governmental Ramakrishna Mission. India is an important donor to the Colombo Plan and has offered training and educational facilities to many underdeveloped countries. Indian sympathy for anti-colonialism and anti-imperialism and for secularism is well known. People are becoming supranational in a true managerial sense because they have begun to see a future of hope and peace through regional groupings and good neighbourly internationalism. Even India and Pakistan momentarily forget their mutual fears and antagonisms when they share the forum of South Asian Association for Regional Co-operation (SAARC). The superpowers are also waking up to the downward drift of mutual deterrents to their own destruction and are now listening to the slogans of emancipation of the world from nuclear weapons or all national stockpiles of weapons. Eventually, until man is not fully evolved in non-violence, some police action will have to be allowed to the international community through the United Nations and its organs. There is now talk of collective security for the entire world.

The internationalism that now sweeps the world is totally different from the emotional internationalism of old times that only reflected aggressive intentions and invited conflicts, like the international struggle for the liberation of the holy places from the Turks during the crusades or the international upsurge in favour of the Caliphate after the First World War. The supranationalism of the Jews as alleged by Hitler was only to malign them so that Hitler gets sympathy from nationalists. 'The workers of the world unite' slogan of Lenin, Stalin and Mao must have been untruthful when we see the aftermath of Stalin and Mao in these countries. The slogan in fact has expanded in scope to include the peace-loving people of all nations who have formed the United Nations. The United Nations is fully alive to its responsibility for victory in the struggle against repression or injustice as in South Africa or Palestine. In a subsequent section we return to the importance of the United Nations for a peaceful world with some machinery for the prevention of conflicts.

2

CONTROVERSIAL ISSUES

Introduction

IF WE observe insects, birds and animals, their existence is beset with interspecie conflicts. Within a specie too, conflict often emerges for the sake of leadership, for mates or just for cockiness. Such conflicts are resolved by acceptance of or obedience to a recognized leader or by obedience to rules laid down by instinct. An ant colony is an example of absence of conflict, though the ants do suffer from attacks from outside and even the ant-eater levies a heavy toll. Joint families or small tribes had well-regulated inter-relationships since there was implicit obedience to the elders or the leaders. There was, however, no external security. Feudal lords overran villages and there was pillage and loot.

History is full of fraternal conflicts for inheritance or leadership and many a kingdom got fragmented due to such fraternal claims. The kaleidoscopic parting and coming together of petty kingdoms did not matter too much to the simple and hard life of the peasant. The State had no other duty but to preserve the rulers in relative ease and comfort. The nation States have come into being with the participation of the people. The welfare of the people and distributing the benefits of increased production and services to all has become the national pre-occupation. For these results, a rational approach eschewing conflicts is necessary.

The 30-year war in the 17th century devastated the whole of Europe when armies marched across its length and breadth. The whole mode of life of the middle ages was shattered. India is also suffering from sudden bursts of conflagration in this or that part of the country which is not good for stability or strength. Resolution of conflict does not imply knuckling down to the threats or acceptance of suicidal dictates from the recalcitrants. People have rightly dealt with a heavy hand the recent revivalist interest in the custom of *Sati* or self-immolation by widows on the funeral pyre of the dead husband. A righteous cause is one which aims at benefits to certain affected people and which does not weaken the nation as a whole. A part of the body cannot be pampered against the health of the whole.

Man's functioning is at a higher plane than that of an animal. He has values like truth, forgiveness, hospitality, etc. Man is equipped with culture and conscience. His values may need support of authority, scriptures or supervision. Children and siblings have conflicts which get resolved through their playmates and elders. The police and the courts may be necessary to control conflicts when these burst into the open. It is, however, far better to re-channel the energy leading to conflicts into constructive tasks and providing opportunities for fair competition. From analogy with the old-fashioned joint family, conflict resolution could perhaps be a new professional task entrusted to some experienced and respected individuals who could be approached by any complaining group for sympathy and advice. This kind of step would be quite in line with modern developments in psycho-therapy. Unfortunately the usual channels for redressal, the police stations and courts with lawyers and professional witnesses, are only interested in fuelling further the fires of conflict as most have an axe to grind. Most sectarian leaders and politicians also get set on one side or the other of the issues. What we require is not analytical talent but arbitrators who can satisfy both sides.

Sometimes a belief takes root that a certain region is denied modernization, health or other services because of regional discrimination. The true reasons for the continued backwardness may be quite obvious like the resources crunch and the suspicion against all personnel from outside the region. Another cause of strife is the neglect of a minority language when the minority is concentrated in a certain district. This means considerable hardship to the minority in communicating with the authorities or in taking advantage of much information readily available in the language of the majority.

There are also the usual class conflicts generated by the mixed pattern of economy and blind consumerism enveloping the cities beckoning to the dispossessed of the villages.

Border Regions

Usually there is the same language or cultural group astride the State or national borders unless there has been deliberate migration or a forced one of the minority across the border. Though religious minorities were compelled to migrate across the borders when Pakistan was formed, still Sindhi, Punjabi and Bengali languages were common across its borders when it was formed. For States within the country such a migration is unthinkable in view of the meaning of nationality. Sometimes migrations are engineered by organized forces notwithstanding the official national policies. Such a recent migration has been of the Chakmas, from across the Bangladesh border into Tripura State of India. When the minority on the wrong side of the border is substantial, we come across bids for autonomy, if not outright rebellion for secession. Soviet republics of Azerbaijan and Armenia have a similar problem, now being sorted out by the grant of autonomy to the Armenians living within the borders of Azerbaijan. There has been a similar problem of large numbers of Nepalis living in Darjeeling district of West Bengal adjoining Nepal, and the solution of granting an autonomous development council to Darjeeling district seems to be acceptable to all concerned. Suppression of the minority culture as a national policy is now discredited. This has been attempted though not very often. A recent example was the Siamization of the Malay minority in south Thailand.

Disquiet near borders leads quickly to insurgency conditions because of succour from across the borders. The insurgents or rebellious terrorists can easily get sanctuaries, regrouping centres, weapons and additional recruits from across the borders. This happened in the case of border States in the east especially Nagaland, Mizoram and Tripura. The Nagaland and Mizoram liberators were eventually satisfied with full statehood status within the Indian Union and have become supporters of the all-India Congress Party. Tripura has a democratically elected government like any other State and the terrorists had Marxist-revolutionary pretensions which have subsided in view of the apathy of the public which freely took part in State elections. The example of democratically elected leftist governments in certain Indian States is also taking the wind out of the sails of revolutionaries. In addition, the USSR and China no longer press for Communist revolutions in other countries. A recalcitrant group (United Libration Front of Assam) is still active on the path of terrorism and violence.

Terrorism in the Punjab

The problem of terrorists in the border State of the Punjab is rather complex. Since the rebellious groups are not at all representing the wishes of the Punjabis or even of a sizable minority of the Punjabis, they are staking their lives for their own 17th century style rule where the power will be with their nominees seated on the religious seats of the Sikhs. The Sikhs in the recent past have had their religious movements through their Akali party. Akalis got enacted through the British Indian Government and then by the national government laws establishing a managing committee of religious shrines, elected under government auspices by voters belonging to the Sikh faith and sporting the five symbols of membership in the faith particularly unshorn beard. The Akalis realized that the Sikh communal vote will not give them the legislative majority to rule the Punjab since the Punjab after partition and merger of princely states of the area had about 50 per cent non-Sikh population. They, thus, started agitating for a *Punjabi Suba* which was a euphemism for a Sikh majority state. The agitation was strictly run on a linguistic basis and contiguous districts of Hindi-speaking majority merged into Himachal Pradesh or formed a new State of Haryana. The few remaining districts became the new Punjab with about 70 per cent Sikh majority. The Akalis then fought few elections as a political party not necessarily of the Sikhs alone. They had success for a short while but again were left in the opposition as the Congress party succeeded in winning majority of the seats through their Hindu and Sikh combined vote bank.

Now the Akalis gave up their democratic pretensions and more and more took up a fascist religious stance. The Anandpur Sahib resolution, adopted by the Akalis as their belief, speaks only of the aimed special position of the Sikhs so that in the Punjab there should be Sikh rule or rule of a semi-theocratic nature where the chief minister and others being Sikhs will give priority to the orders from the Sikh shrine irrespective of the mandate, if any, from the legislature. They started agitations one after the other aiming at a confrontation with the Congress rule in the Punjab and also the national government at the centre, accusing the national government of being a Hindu-dominated government in exactly the same style as that of the pre-partition Muslim League. An often repeated charge was that the Sikhs are discriminated against whereas many high official positions were occupied by the Sikhs through their own ability. India has also other religious minorities like the Parsis or the Christians who are few in numbers like the Sikhs, but who had no such complaint.

The Akalis also tagged on some local complaints like insufficient central funds being invested in the Punjab and the waters of the rivers which gave the name to the State being treated as a common national resource, etc. In this environment of agitation and budding religio-fascist movement in negation of the secular democratic principles of Indian revolution and freedom, all kinds of adventurism stepped in. It is firmly believed that the Punjabi faction of the Congress party in an attempt to out-do Herod created Bhindranwale who promoted extremism much beyond the Akali Anandpur resolution. He declared that in the Punjab only Sikhs must rule and establish a Khalistan which will pursue imperialist policies of the ancient Sikh State. Hindus were a lower species than the Sikhs who had long ago given up Hinduism and rebelled against the Central rule from Delhi (Mughal empire) in the 17th and 18th centuries. It was now relatively easy to project the national government at Delhi as the direct successor of the Mughals out to commit atrocities on the Sikhs and the State government, with the Sikh chief minister as representing only the weak and numerically less significant Sikhs, to the illiterate Sikh masses through the weekly harangues by the Sikh priests from the Gurdwaras.

Bhindranwale was the first Sikh leader to organize systematic terror against all national and local moderate leadership. There was repudiation of Bhindranwale by both the Congress and the Akalis. The law and order machinery broke down. The State government was suspended and Punjab's rule passed on direct to the Central government as per the constitutional provisions. Now the border position of the State played its part. The fugitive terrorists found easy access to foreign countries through the co-operation of Pakistan and many Sikh settlers in the U.K., Canada and the USA. The Sikh settlers abroad had amassed great wealth and were carried away by the stories of Central government repression of the Sikhs as their own knowledge of pre-partition India was when communal labels were very important in India. They were willing to support the establishment of a Sikh homeland in India carried away by the example of Zionism that established a Jewish homeland in Palestine. These expatriate Sikhs living in democratic societies but perhaps suffering some racial indignities there equated the condition of the Sikhs with that of the European Jews. It is very much on the cards that certain forces in these countries not well disposed to growing Indian influence in the United

Nations encouraged the terrorist conspiracy of Bhindranwale's followers. To sum-up large sums of money and large quantities of weapons were smuggled into the Punjab and recruitment of terrorists was carried out in complicity with certain powerful elements of Pakistan. When Bhindranwale entrenched himself in the *Akal Takht* and the Golden Temple at Amritsar and was liquidated, the so-called sensible Sikh leaders even became off-balance. They wailed that Bhindranwale should not have been killed with his followers in the Golden Temple but should have been held earlier when he had just started getting notoriety.

The extermination of the terrorists in the temple was called an attack on their Jerusalem — house of God. The tempers ran high and the Indian prime minister, (Mrs.) Indira Gandhi, became a martyr to the secular principles of India. This was followed by angry demonstrations and wanton killing of innocent Sikh citizens by Delhi hooligans justifying their lust for loot and violence by the open celebration, of Indira Gandhi's murder, by some Sikhs in the Capital. Later the glorification of Indira Gandhi's assassins as martyrs by the *Akal Takht* resulted in Jammu riots.

There was clamour on all sides for retrieval of the worsening situation and Sant Longowal, the president of the Akali Dal, and Rajiv Gandhi, newly appointed prime minister, boldly entered into the Rajiv-Longowal Pact seeking to re-install a democratically-elected government in the Punjab. An Akali ministry representing in principle all Punjabis and not just the Sikhs was formed, though the chief minister did not include any non-Sikh in his ministry. The terrorists, however, were not to be thwarted, they continued to murder peasants, professional people, religious leaders (including Longowal), intellectuals (including Tewari), priests both Hindu and Sikh who might speak out the truth that the Sikhs were the culmination of the Hindu tradition in *Bhakti* and philosophy and most Hindus and Sikhs were having close family ties with each other. There have been instances of heroic mutual protection of Hindus and Sikhs and cowardly terrorist attacks on women and children or sneak attacks on unarmed men of piety and insight. There has been considerable retrogress in Punjab's commerce though the government has invested large sums in new industries. The terrorist killings will end only when Pakistan withdraws its support and helps India in the control of border crime of smuggling narcotics, etc., that allows the common criminals of both the countries to do business with the terrorists who have brainwashed recruits who are literally paid employees for any dare-devilry. There is plenty of money from overseas and from extortions in the Punjab for the mayhem.

The long-range solution lies with the leadership of the Sikhs, in religious matters or otherwise, to see the advantages of a secular State and to keep religion separate from politics since India is the home of many religions and co-existence alone suits Indian progress. Often it is the local politicians who out of autistic fears blindly raise suicidal slogans which are against the local interests in the long run and certainly against the national interests of the whole country comprising many communities and creeds. While the Sikhs have an honoured place in the country in every walk of life and the Punjab, where the majority of population is Sikh, has the highest per capita income in India and where a democratically elected government whether of Congress party or a party of the opposition has operated without any controversy with the Central Government, the slogans regarding discrimination and special status for Sikhs, who are one of the many communities residing in India, are simply unfair and a throw-back to the dark era of oppression and slavery in the country. People, who either do not believe in democracy or want it to work only in their favour, have no patience to woo the public to choose them as their spokesmen. They soon take to agitations and violence or evoke response which is oppressive from the authorities. The law and order suffer. The same happened when J.P. desired a total revolution in the country without the processes of education and building up of a following for revolutionary ways. The agitations and disturbances ended in emergency and induction of evil means in government counsels.

Mahatma Gandhi declared that a civilization will be judged by its treatment of the minorities. The Sikh terrorists of the Punjab are idealizing themselves as Zionists out to create a homeland for the 'oppressed' Sikhs of the Punjab where ironically they being the majority can form the elected government. And they wish to treat the Hindu minority of the Punjab as the Jewish minority in Nazi Germany, i.e. they should have no rights and are pontifically declared unfit as rulers compared to Sikhs, while historically Punjab Hindus have been behind none else in the exercise of authority or command even under the rule of Maharaja Ranjit Singh in the Punjab, whose well-known military commanders included Punjab Hindus. Banda Bahadur, a Hindu, won the only Sikh victory before the success of Maharaja

Ranjit Singh and also made the supreme sacrifice for the Punjabis. The oppression of Jews in Germany was by the majority for rooting out racial differences literally. Most fundamentalist oppressions on the national scale belong to this category. Unfortunately this kind of regional majority chauvinism is presented to the world at large including expatriate Sikhs as struggle by a religious minority for rights which, they feel, are their due, notwithstanding what other majorities and minorities may feel. In a secular democratic multi-state country, there is no room for thinking in terms of communal majority and minority. The doctrine perfected by fascists of oppression of minority should hold no attraction to communal minorities in India, but unfortunately they seem to hug such inhuman ideas in districts or areas where they happen to form the majority community. Not necessarily the whole community is so misguided but initially they allowed the Bhindranwale types considerable latitude.

The Akalis were very much in the forefront of opposition to the Nirankaris whose only fault was that following the original Hindu tradition they believe in a living Guru who can guide them in following the written word of the great Gurus. Even if this belief does not conform to the teaching of the tenth Guru, it cannot be held as abominable. Guru Nanak openly differed from the religious practices of his times whether Hindu or Muslim but was universally respected for the sincerity of his beliefs. Part of the blame goes to the Indian political leadership unilaterally agreeing to give special status to the State of Jammu and Kashmir as some States now wish to have similar status. Jammu and Kashmir is a Muslim majority State but not a Muslim homeland like Pakistan or an Islamic State. Due to special circumstances, it has considerable autonomy and has a separate Constitution besides being an autonomous State in the Indian Union, a sort of model of federating states in case India chooses eventually to be a federation of States and not as at present a unitary State with some powers decentralized to the component States.

Ladakh and Tamil Eelam

We shall consider two other international border areas: one in J&K and the other in Sri Lanka, since the problems are of concern to India. Ladakh is the border region with China and the Indo-Chinese boundary is in dispute. Ladakh is almost cold desert with very little agriculture. Only recently wind power and solar energy have been harnessed to aid agriculture by scientists of BARC, CSIR, etc. Ladakhis form a Buddhist minority in J&K and their complaint is about uncontrolled arrival of outsiders from J&K. They also feel neglected like other hill areas regarding their share of development projects. They had considerable trade with Tibet and this was disrupted due to the occupation of Tibet by China, though now some border trade is again allowed. Recently the aim of being declared a protected area in J&K has been accepted and Ladakhis are settling down to a period of progress. Indo-Tibetan trade is also picking up.

India has also got involved in the suppression of Tamil rebellion in the Northern and the Eastern parts of Sri Lanka where Tamils constitute the majority, though Tamils are scattered all over Sri Lanka. Like the Sikhs of the Punjab, Tamils desired the rest of Sri Lanka to be secular and democratic but for themselves an independent State (Tamil Eelam) in the northern and eastern parts of the country. There were charges and counter-charges of communalism. In 1984 there were violent anti-Tamil riots in Tamil minority areas and as a reaction as well as in continuation of separatist policies of certain sections of Tamils, an active virulent rebellion broke out in Tamil majority areas followed by brutal repression by the Sri Lankan government driving away thousands of refugees into the Tamil Nadu State of India. The revolt continued and could not be suppressed. Sri Lankan forces were becoming ineffective and Sri Lanka sought assistance from outsiders like Israeli terrorist agencies, etc. These agencies were not well disposed to India. India was saddled with a large refugee population who were becoming a law and order problem in India and excited Indian Tamils against so-called inaction of the Indian Government. Slowly the Sri Lankan media started charging India with aiding and abetting the Tamils. India all along declared her commitment to the national integrity of Sri Lanka and desired the parties to arrive at a negotiated settlement. Slowly Indian intentions were believed by the Sri Lankan government and Rajiv-Jayawardene agreement was signed seeking to establish a regional council for the Tamil regions within Sri Lanka. India claims that the agreement was arrived at with the verbal concurrence and full discussion with the Tamil leadership including leaders of the Liberation Tigers of Tamil Eelam (LTTE) which is in the forefront of the Tamil rebellion. India was to send Indian Peace Keeping Force (IPKF) into Tamil regions of Sri Lanka and accept surrender of arms from the Tamil rebels. Most Tamils of the region accepted the agreement with relief, but after some time the LTTE, measuring Indian policies with their own standard of fulfilling agreements, refused to surrender arms and in fact tried to augment recruits and its cache of arms by liquidating all opposition and planning a dictatorship once the IPKF quit or became lethargic. As a consequence the Indian forces in Sri Lanka were engaged in liquidating the LTTE terrorists and snatching arms from them. Slowly the tide is turning and the diehards are surrendering having lost all sympathy of the Tamil public especially because the Sri Lankan government is seen to be meticulously fulfilling their part of the Rajiv-Jayawardene accord and soon the autonomous council for Tamil majority areas will be effective and the whole country will be governed on secular democratic lines. Unfortunately, after the withdrawal of IPKF, the rebellion and violent suppression has again flared up, but inexorably the, negotiated settlement is coming nearer. Here is a classic example of an attempt at conflict resolution by the patient counselling as well as buttressed by armed authority of a third party. Similarly, the USA and the Soviet Union have come to an agreement to leave the Afghanistan problem to Afghan devices alone and not to send armies to support any of the minority factions: the Communist government in Kabul or the Mujahideen taking refuge in Pakistan who are a sizable force matching the Afghan government forces. The good offices of the U.N. Secretary General were used during the negotiated settlement, but the Secretary General is not counting on any force to enforce agreement by the parties or on the guarantors. Already there are Russian accusations that the Mujahideen are not returning when invited back by the Afghan government but are spoiling for a fight since they are continuing to get supplies of arms and other aid from the West and the Pakistani authorities. The solution lies in the establishment of a true democratic secular State and not in any factional victory of the fundamentalists or the Communists. There has to be a broad-based government to which at least the government of the Communists is now inclined, but an effective supervisory force may still be needed for the interim period to enforce ceasefire and elections.

Demand for Autonomous Districts

Some districts of certain States are economically backward primarily because of the hilly terrain and lack of communications and infra-structure. Such a situation needs special attention which the

States are unable to devote because of many factors, e.g. lack of strong lobby advocating the case of the backward area since they lack education, skills and political muscle. These areas in the past were allowed to stay backward being the playgrounds of princes and the rich gentry of the plains. There was also the Nehru gospel advising least interference with tribals who must develop at their own pace not relinquishing their quaint ways and customs. But with increased spread of communications, radio and television, the backward areas are no longer contented with their lot. The development of the tribal and hill areas certainly requires more skill and help than just neglect. The policy now is of declaring such backward areas as autonomous districts or, if the population affected and the area are large enough, of declaring them to be a separate Union Territories or new States so that their own elected representatives can look after their management. In the past the neglect has often bred dacoits and anarchists in these jungles or barren areas, hence the new policy is very timely. There will be special provisions for communications, education and forest management, etc. The effort is augmented by voluntary agencies now particularly active in the tribal belts of Maharashtra and Gujarat. Special forest departmental programmes are launched in Bastar district, Telengana and the tribal belts of Bihar and Orissa, which have been most exploited by organized criminals.

The country is now alive to the approaching ecological disaster if the rape of natural forests is not immediately checked and proper management installed in place of present activity of licences for exploitation. The tribal folk who snatch a precarious living from forests can be relied upon to help preserve the forests given the proper guidance and results of modern researches. The Chipko movement that started from grassroots for preservation of individual trees was the first one to draw the national attention to the problem of uncontrolled activities of the contractors in league with corrupt or lethargic forest officials and politicians. Indeed the management of forests and catchment areas is of utmost importance for saving the country from floods and droughts. Local initiative has to be harnessed by political action. SAARC has studied the co-operative development of the Himalayan region and of the marine resources and all countries of South Asia will benefit by such co-operation. The conflict of the hill and forest dwellers with the rest of the country is because of inactivity in application of modern methods of forest and pasture management or of fisheries development in the remote areas with relatively hard living conditions for the non-residents who are not allowed to strike root, but who have to be used as change agents.

Minority Rights

Earlier only a small apex minority had all the rights and the great majority was either of low caste or were serfs or slaves with few rights. The ancient values were replaced by new values of equal human rights before the power structure of society changed. The culture and the religion of the powerful apex group became the preferred religion, especially in Europe. The nations of Europe first experienced communalism and communal conflicts and the rights of the religious community other than the one wielding power became constitutionally as well as by custom reduced. Gypsies though in majority in many towns of Slovakia suffered from anti-Gypsy bias in housing under segregationist pressures. In spite of professed political philosophy of equality before law, the fragmentation of polity in terms of majority and minority religious groups developed. In common understanding, minority refers to religious minority. When ideas of modern democracy were grafted on to the Indian scene, the concept of religious majority and minority was also imported. Before the advent of British rule, the kings safeguarded only their own position and rarely differentiated between subjects of different communities and the so-called majority and minority religions had mutual respect for faith and piety, there being never any recorded purely communal conflict. When the British found warring factions in India, they mistook these as arising from the religious differences. And since factionalism suited them, everyone was assigned a permanent majority or minority status and mutual suspicions were fanned. Thus, political competition was deliberately structured along religious lines. Even decades after independence, people are still concerned with fears of religious majority or aggression by some religious minority or the other, in spite of adult suffrage and giving up of separate electorates based on religious labels. A class of politicians wish to use the priests, etc., of every religion, who have the ear of the populace in order to perpetuate mutual religious majority-minority suspicions and fears, for retaining control of the country in their hands. Often the elections are clandestinely fought on religious appeal even though exciting religious sentiments for winning an election is illegal. The loaves and fishes of office are claimed on the basis of belonging to certain community supposedly less represented in any particular office. The feelings regarding injustice because of belonging to a minority community often lie only in the mind of the individual. In India, family linkages and loyalty even to chance acquaintances are strong. Favouritism and choosing employees on the basis of expected personal loyalty, because of family or familiar connections, are universal in private business and industry. This is taken as preference being given to majority community while the same will apply if the business or industry were being controlled by a member of the minority community. Though selection of personnel can be made objective eliminating all bias, yet it happens to sway most selections and in very high positions it is usually in favour of the minority communities.

With modernization when more and more specialists will be required and will be available, there is likely to be selection on an objective basis, purely on merit for the progress of any business or industry in an increasingly competitive environment. Already accounting, marketing and management are slipping from mere friends and relations to professionally qualified and technologically competent persons.

Majority-minority friction is exacerbated by senseless jokes. Just like rumours, such jokes are invented by clever brain-washers and propagated by short-sighted people usually of the other community. This should be nipped in the bud by deliberate education of children in good manners and training them to respect diversity which is the prime fact of existence in India. The common Sardarji and Marwari jokes are in fact an appreciation of their success in particular spheres which were so difficult apparently for others. There should, however, be conscious effort by anecdotes, etc., to disseminate the good points of members of a minority community. Though Sardarjis and Punjabis are often projected as quarrelsome, but in actual fact so many instances of altruistic action by them would be available. Diverse groups must be instructed in elements of evolution of culture, nature of superstition, scientific approach and rudiments of philosophy in the efforts towards integration of our society in its diversity.

Prosperity seems to make people isolationist. Our well-to-do pockets like Hyderabad, Bombay and now the villages of Punjab are so jealous of their prosperity that they are reluctant to share it with job seekers from other States. They want to discriminate against outsiders like the British or the Australians might do. In spite of the overt or covert ill-will against the outsiders, fast developing economies invite and attract suitable immigrants. Our isolationists in Assam, J&K, Bombay, etc., should also understand the economics of immigrant labour. If necessary, they can appoint annual immigration quotas in consideration of the annual emigration to other States and other countries as well as needs of special skills and manpower not readily available locally. By being hostile to advantageous immigration, they only harm themselves and be stumbling blocks in national integration that helps all. If a census is taken, it will be seen, for example, that more people have left Manipur for greener pastures than have entered the State in the last five years. Imagine the absurdity of Punjab terrorists murdering daily wage labourers from Bihar who are so valuable to the farmers as seasonal labour and have no intention or plan to settle permanently in the Punjab. The advantage of belonging to a large nation is to have the opportunity to seek advancement in any part of the large country and to count on the availability of material and energy resources, far and near for implementation of one's own regional or district plans. In fact, along with acceptance of planned immigration from other States there should be assistance forthcoming to planned emigration to other places which were in the habit of counting on such immigration. The different Indian languages could be taught to prospective emigrants for better utilization of manpower which is the greatest resource of India for development. From now on Indian embassies should take an active interest in the development plans of African States and offer timely assistance of trained manpower conversant with the language and culture of those countries.

Besides religious minorities, there are linguistic minorities. Even when Indian States were reorganized on the basis of language, linguistic minorities continued to live in all States. Every minority language cannot be the language of administration in each and every district. The multi-lingual formula alone is the answer. The linguistic minorities have caught hold of the language issue from the wrong angle. The minority language is not really threatened by the language of the majority, but by the continued expansion in coverage by the entirely foreign English language. A linguistic synthesis of 'Vishwa Karma' language based on spoken and TV/Radio idiom and using phonetic version of the Roman script will go a long way in solving the Indian language problems. Every new textbook of science and medicine or new technological institute should begin developing and using the new 'Vishwa Karma' language so that the English language does not get entrenched deeper and international vocabulary of science and technology is literally appropriated just as the composite Indo-Persian culture gave birth to Urdu. The scientific advancement of the country is handicapped for want of a broad-based language.

Language Issue

It is doubtful if any other country in the whole world has had language riots of the type Tamil Nadu or the State of Uttar Pradesh had the unique distinction to have. Violent mobs attacked signboards, mile posts, etc., written in the wrong alphabet. Even international numerals written in standard form were not spared. The languages are now associated in general with distinct States, e.g. Punjabi, Gujarati, Marathi, Tamil, Telegu, Kanarese, Bengali, Kashmiri, etc. Near the borders of each State there is a linguistic minority often having substantial numbers in one or two districts. The secondary school medium of instruction usually is the State language, though primary education is generally assured in the mother-tongue. Where the primary education is not available in the mother-tongue or if in a district, government notices and court summons are not published in the minority language, there is agitation almost for secession favourable to the State across the borders. Such a problem has arisen in the Bellary district of Maharashtra. Redrawing of State boundaries is not feasible since such linguistic minority problems are in all States and no amount of redrawing of boundaries can eliminate these. The solution lies in maximum districtwise decentralization and by allowing secondary schools in such districts the option to affiliate to the school board of the neighbouring State. The inter-State constitutional board, set up for solving inter-State and Centre-State issues, will perhaps sort out such problems by discussions with the Centre as a third party assisting negotiations. There has been a major north-south controversy within India on the issue of a national language for India. Constitutionally the majority voted for Hindi as the national language, but there was no consensus on a single language. Since the bureaucracy and the ruling elite were carrying on their work generally in English from the colonial days and the southern States were more afraid of Hindi imperialism than continued slavery of the entire country to the English language, in the consensus English was allowed to have the status and functioning of a national language for 15 years in the first instance but the provision has been silently continued and it seems to suit no set of politicians to terminate the national status of

English. The language riots broke out when the first 15 years were over. It was decided that the decision regarding the national language would be taken only with the concurrence of southern States and thus English continued. It is in fact entrenching itself. All science and technology, medicine and engineering are carried out in English. A person not having the knowledge of English can perhaps become a politician or a journalist or an artist or a poet, but can hardly accomplish much in any other field. Often, in the job market, he is considered illiterate or mere assistant and technician and paid one-third of what an English-knowing person of similar calibre would get. There is now a vested interest of the bureaucracy and the ruling class in the continuation of English. The advanced education with translation of modern technology and management terms for certain Indian language universities flopped in the face of competition from the English-knowing candidates.

Not that the Indian elite did not have a national language in the past. Up to recent times Sanskrit was understood by all learned people, especially the Pandits who were scattered at the rate of at least one family per village all over the country. In the times of the Mughal empire, the feudal aristocracy, mainly Muslim and Rajput, developed Urdu as a national language, besides the use of Sanskrit and Persian. Hindi and Urdu practically developed together, the main difference being the use of Persian script for Urdu and Devnagri script for Hindi. Urdu used words borrowed freely from Sanskrit, Hindi, Persian and Turkish dialects. Urdu literally meant the language of the military camp. Hindu priests continued to use Sanskrit but the common people understood it less and less. The Muslim *mullahs* continued to intone the *Koran* in Arabic, but they were understood less and less in Arabic. In analogy with the history of the national language for the last few hundred years, perhaps the language of choice will be Hindi/Urdu written in Roman script with a liberal sprinkling of English words especially to make the new Vishwa Karma language a fit vehicle for technology institutes and the common vehicle for science education. The creative energies of the Indian people are still latent because literature in science is only in English and even the scientists cannot spread the scientific method among the populace as they are innocent of any common dialect.

It is time that all States realize that the struggle for a State language is not with Hindi but with English which is slowly entrenching itself in the education of infants to the education of highest knowledge of science, technology, engineering, medicine and management in the country and there is growing vested interest in it of the elite of India while the large mass is condemned to ignorance of advanced knowledge. We are afraid that as a reaction the non-English-knowing masses may not throw away the modern knowledge along with the English-knowing ruling elite like throwing away the baby with the bath water. From now on there should be planned effort to use and spread the new Vishwa Karma language to replace English as the medium of new knowledge in India. No one is propagating against the various State languages or Hindi and Urdu for literature, various newspapers and poetic works. The religious books can continue in their existing idiom and scripts. About a century ago the Germans replaced German script by Roman script for strictly scientific and technical works so that they were widely appreciated in Europe. We must do some similar sacrifice for national integration and spread of the scientific method and its easy acceptance in all parts of the country since all Indians have already become so familiar with the Roman alphabet and international numerals. A similar device has been used in the Russian Muslim minority region by Latinization of Arabic with profuse use of Russian scientific terms.

SC/ST Privileges for Government Employment

Indian society has been neglecting the progress of a large section of people comprising the scheduled castes and scheduled tribes. The Indian privileged castes have literally exploited these groups almost like slaves or ones ordained to do their bidding. The national leaders after Independence and considerable spade work, done by the Congress and other revolutionary and reformist movements in the country, desired society to make some amends for the past misdeeds. A special quota in all levels of jobs was fixed for them and thus SC/ST candidates get admission to advanced professional institutes, etc., out of turn as well as get government or public sector jobs reserved for them both at the entry or promotion points. The public in general supported such measures. Now, after 40 years, since the application of such privileges, people wish to take stock of the situation and want justice as all citizens of the country are equal in the eyes of law and deserve equality of opportunity. Fairly well-to-do families from SC/ST label continue to enjoy the benefit of such rules while others even of better merit suffer. A promotion of a less qualified person on whatever basis demoralizes others. Similarly, admission to a medical college or engineering college to a less apt pupil disconcerts other young minds. The concessions should have been limited to certain period while the average person of these castes and tribes picked up sufficient self-respect and ability to compete with others. Instead such privileges have unfortunately been extended by certain States and managements to all kinds of classes, like wards of men of various prominence or various states of indigence. There seems to be no satiation in legalized patronage. All such privileges must be done away with. However, certain economically backward people, including SC and ST, do deserve some support. The support should be for a restricted number of years, say, 30, i.e. one or two generations of children by giving them liberal education grants and special (pre-entrance examination or previous to open competitions) coaching, so that they are brought up to the general requirements of appearing in the tests. Once provision is made for their special coaching, they should be entirely left to compete on their own merit and ability. The army has sometimes carried out such coaching and assistance to candidates with rural background to bring them up to the level of city-bred candidates in general knowledge and deportment. When one is already employed, promotion must be earned by merit alone. Similarly, merit scholarships must not mean any distinction regarding the income of guardians (the merit-cum-means scholarships could be a separate category). The intelligence and ability must not be diluted to avoid the double disadvantage of saddling the services with inefficiency and spreading discontentment among normal hard-working employees. There is a danger that a permanent policy of concessions for correcting inequality may create a new inequality.

Sons of the Soil Theory

Many of our eastern States have adopted the provisions, like those of J&K, of not allowing Indian nationals of other States to acquire property and to be put on the electoral rolls in such States. Some States and also the vociferous spokesmen of large cities like Hyderabad of Andhra Pradesh and Bombay of Maharashtra would not allow any outsider to earn a living in their rich cities. If unchecked, such regional ambitions would reduce Indian citizenship to a liability than be a matter of pride. Only against the superior enterprise and self-interest of an outsider, should the locals be enabled to safeguard their ecology and farmland or the unplanned exploitation of the natural resources. In the interest of all-round development, each region should properly look at its skills and requirements and control intelligently its emigration and immigration even from the rest of India. The advantage of being nationals of a single large rich country should not be lost due to unintelligent grasp of the present. An Indian citizen, deciding to settle in a State different from his own, is an integrating link and must be made very welcome with no discrimination of any kind. Even the isolationist sentiment in J&K will diminish with time when they meet all along a welcome from the rest of the country and, being primarily a great tourist resort, it already has welcomed enterprise and increased tourist flow from the rest of the country. The people must also learn to appreciate the culture and activities of the host population. The fundamentalist debacle in Iran-Iraq conflict, the dictatorship proneness in the Islamic State of Pakistan will slowly bring home once again to the populace the superior merit of secularism and democracy. In fact, J&K leaders were the original tested secularists in the country among the communal minority labels. The parochial clamour has to be guided back to integrationism by guaranteeing equality of opportunity in the whole country along with protection of natural resources and husbanding of farmland, forests and ecology in general.

Family Strife

People not only encounter politico-religious differences but are often beset with family strife. Mahabharata war destroyed India of old because of family envy and jealousy. Many tribes have been feuding up to recent times. Some of the terrorist killings in the Punjab are results of family enmities. The dissatisfaction with the share in inheritance or usurpation of inheritance by aggressive relatives leads to considerable complaints, litigation or private violence. An ideal solution of social significance would be reversion of all property after demise to the local custodian appointed by a local representative body or by the government and the legal heirs to be given some reasonable support not out of proportion to the means at the disposal of others of similar background. The means of production, like land or factory, should not go to heirs without proper social say-so. Any surplus, after meeting the liabilities of the deceased and reasonable provision for the heirs, should be managed contractually in common social interest. From ancient times most of the tilled land belonged to God or King and the tiller had only tenancy rights. It cannot be justified that in a socialist pattern of society the rich man's heirs have a head start over others by inheriting vast wealth and businesses. Abolishment of the estate duties is a capitalist step in our mixed economy, because the government has begun to trust the efficiency of private enterprise more than that of the government bureaucracy and would rather allow the private persons to have more accumulated wealth. A cause for future strife is going to be the new law equating sons and daughters in the matter of inheritance. This is not quite logical though we would like that the law and practice are impartial between sons and daughters.

In common practice the father looks after the son till he starts earning. Then the father and the son start having a joint family and the son looks after the old parents. The daughter is looked after till her marriage when she starts living with her husband as an added member of the husband's father's household. If she earns, it goes to the new household. She or her husband has no social obligation to look after her parents in their old age. In equity to all concerned, the daughter's share should be evaluated at the time of her marriage and rupee equivalent be paid to her without further interest within, say, two years of the marriage in mutually convenient instalments and the balance, if any, should later carry the usual bank interest. The property accruing to the parents after the daughter's marriage will not provide any share to the daughter who will have had her equal share earlier. The immovable property will also not be fragmented avoiding any problems of involving a different family in the management of land/factories, etc., of the daughter's parents. One of the reasons advanced by the Akalis before the Punjab agitations was the new provision for fragmentation of land through the equal share of the daughter later living in a different family, perhaps of a different village, at the death of the father. The method suggested above will also do away with the evils of the giving and taking of dowry, since the exact monetary portion to be accruing to the daughter within two years of marriage will be well known and dowry seekers will look elsewhere for the daughter of a richer father. The method suggested above will endow daughters with dignity and they will have no occasion to suffer jibes for insufficient dowry. Disproportionate expectations and lies would cease. Since the marriage will no longer be a plunge in uncertainty and the bridegroom and his parents will have no say in the management of the property of daughter's parents or brothers, the conflicts and cruelty to brides will cease. Once objectivity and reality is brought in, the climate of greed for more and more and the execution of the hen that lays the golden eggs will cease. After all the dowry system was a revolutionary improvement over the much worse system of payment of bride price by the groom's side in the west or in tribal antiquity. There is also the age-old strife between the spouses when they cannot make a complete success of their married life together. This sometimes leads to divorce which has now begun to be accepted even among the Hindus. The solution would be in humane divorce laws and modernization of expectations from marriage. The ancient value of idolizing of the husband by the wife and contentment in abject service to him has to give way to equality and friendship in marriage. The spouses should do well to listen to friends or elders or if necessary to professional counsellors or the family gurus and *pirs* in the interest of continued happy married life so essential for the proper upbringing of the offspring. Conflict resolution can be a new specialization for religious preachers/priests/psychiatrists/elders to be imposed as counsellors by representative bodies or courts on quarrelling groups and individuals.

Consumer Hardship

The common man is not well-organized to face rackets or bureaucratic high-handedness and inefficiency. Usually complaints reach the sympathetic authority too late, and harassment multiplies. But eventually even a worm will turn. Consumer hardship will bring ridicule to the existing system, thus paving way to dictatorships or then again a newer dictatorship and eventually anarchical conditions. People observe and keep count. Corruption like blood will be out and nemesis cannot be far. There have been near riots for corrupt people stealing electric power in collusion with officials. The terrorists, often in the garb of revolutionary justice, hang corrupt officials and the contractors from the lamp-posts. A major plank of the opposition parties in India is to eliminate corrupt elements entrenched in the government and the national economy. The public listens to all this. Pakistan has proved that a theocracy or military dictatorship only compounds the malady. The increasing difference between the high incomes and the low incomes, the widespread poverty, are signs of profiteering, unethical pricing policies and inefficient production and distribution. The only solution is back-pedalling of high consumerism and doing away with permits and controls in the hands of do-nothing bureaucrats. People had high hopes from the public sector, government-financed co-operative sector and public distribution channels. The benefits were supposed to be passed on to the consumer, but they are being syphoned off by the blue-eyed boys of the political patrons or these fill the coffers of the political parties for their electioneering and for cornering all the positions of profit in society. The best constructive programme for any aspiring political party will be a widespread consumer movement. It was essentially the failure of the distribution system and exploitation through monopolistic pricing that led to the storming of the Bastille and the French Revolution.

3

EXPLOITATION

Introduction

COMPETITION BETWEEN individuals or between industries within permissible limits is healthy. But when it takes the form of personalized immediate antagonism between managements and organized labour, it is an industrial dispute requiring every attention and effort for defusing the situation before the industrial conflict takes an alarming shape in the form of strikes, lock-outs and violence, accompanied by starvation, dismissals, sabotage, etc. The negotiation machinery should be kept alive even during the steepest strife. The usual picture has been the capitalists trying to maximize their profits by keeping the wages as low as possible. The starving labour will be available at cheap rates. In a democratic welfare state, managing a large public sector and public services employing a large number of people, the question of profits through the exploitation of labour should not arise. The exploitation, if any, is because of bureaucratic bungling and the nature of the bourgeoise class determining the management style. There is a built-in bias against the poor and at every step bureaucracy leans back in giving the labour its legitimate due. In the private sector, the neo-capitalism would not cheat the labour of its legitimate dues and they would make profits from the volume of production and improvement in quality to maintain a competitive edge. Low wages go against skilled work and are counter-productive where a sense of responsibility and pride in the quality of one's work is involved.

The common man is exploited on all sides. The police in India has yet to erase the reputation of high-handedness and the tradition for corruption. Banking is often accused of perfecting the money-lender's tricks. People are forced to purchase sub-standard and adulterated stuff. Development and maintenance funds which should benefit all go to fill the coffers of politicians, bureaucrats and corrupt contractors. Before the democratic process entirely fails some safety steps must be taken. The government has done well in providing prompt and cheap redress in certain matters through special tribunals, *Lok Ayukts*, people's courts, *Panchayati Raj*, etc. Such steps should be multiplied. Reliable public workers and tried government servants of integrity after retirement could be encouraged to become change agents or be clothed with authority like the honorary magistrates of old, so that obvious offences can be dealt with summarily, provided an entirely new revolutionary police force is also organized leaving the present one only for ceremonial occasions and for the protection of VIPs. The present-day courts with sworn falsehoods and opposite interpretations of the legal situation from a hierarchy of courts need drastic changes.

Society must recognize class prejudice where it exists and take steps to root it out for controlling exploitation. The exploiting classes first build up prejudice to rationalize the exploitation indulged in, by them. The former untouchables in India, the blacks in the USA, in Brazil or certain outcastes in Japan were the victims of prejudice nourished through generations. Removal of untouchability is partly due to technological and economic advances made by the people in general. Racial prejudice is virulent in South Africa but lurks in many countries. Indians are now suffering from the same in Fiji. This requires special international efforts by India in association with fair-minded people of those countries; and by setting an example of unprejudiced dealings within the country and making minorities and women proud of their country.

Religion and philosophy, police and crime intelligence, teachers and preachers have to be used to remove various kinds of exploitation. Moral education and authority vested in wide-awake people may become necessary. While choosing persons in authority, their philosophy must be probed rather than their desire to amass wealth. At present money power seems to be supreme. Blackmail and dishonesty are quite common even when, from one's position and work, it may not at all be even in one's short-term interest. A straight-forward person is quickly singled out for punishment and first given a bad name for the safety of the herd. It is peculiar to us in India as depicted in the *Ramayana* that a virtuous king is heaped with suffering and a virtuous queen is subjected to fire test and finds refuge only with mother earth. A section of the people were jubilant when Indira Gandhi was murdered and a section of the press was after the scalp of the prime minister. Let us now take heed and invent ways to recognize virtue and efficiency and reward the same. We echo Nehru when he felt that the scientific outlook might rejuvenate the diseased elements of our society especially when religion and philosophy have not been such a big success, in spite of the great philosophical heights which might have been scaled by a few in India.

Labour Movement

Marx and Lenin assigned a revolutionary role to industrial labour since they argued that the industrial labour with their technical and management skills and working in large groups will be a revolutionary class for changing the value system of society in favour of pragmatism. Capitalism had goaded the labour into wage slavery in their chase for profits. Industrialization started in India with coal, railways and textiles and true to their assigned role, industrial labour was in the forefront of the national struggle for independence and for development. The Congress and the communists vied with each other to form and control trade unions. Ahmedabad textile mill workers' strike has been a classic example of peaceful labour struggle. After Independence, the working conditions and wages were improved and often pegged to the price index determined by the government. In the colonial days the managements could depend on the police and the government to support them against organized labour. After Independence the political support was with the labour and managements had often to accept the demands of the unions, often industries fled from communist controlled states. However, soon agitations gave way to negotiations and adjudication. The crunch, however, has come due to soaring inflation and wages are always chasing prices which remain a few steps ahead. The value of money is going down more than the negotiated increase in wages. Production is insufficient to meet the demands of national ambitions on account of modernization already delayed by a century. At the moment the proportion of people below the poverty line is increasing in spite of the fact that a large number have improved their earnings and are prosperous, trying to match the westerners in the mad rush for consumerism. Strikes are pre-empted because of the political support in favour of reasonable wages, but the workers remain unhappy because of ever increasing prices and widespread proportional increase in unemployment of skilled workers.

We have the spectacle of government servants, even the policemen, forming unions, showing dissatisfaction and threatening strikes for more wages. National development means sparing enormous resources for new schemes and, therefore, compelling the nation to save on consumption. The relatively less wage and immunity to disciplinary action in the public sector amounts ultimately to inefficiency. The private industrialist and the bureaucrat have resorted to cheating and falsifying accounts thus creating considerable unaccounted money for their spending. Such spending gives the national economy a queer twist for useless expenditure against the national interest and continuously eggs on others to agitate for more wages or for ill-gotten gains. There is a universal go-slow movement requiring money to oil the machinery of administration in offices. What is necessary is the re-establishment of the cult of work than the ideal of idleness.

The labour laws give all the necessary protection and the government has practically outlawed union activity or strikes from most government offices, providing extensive welfare and participative management. There is cultural ebb in the self-involvement for ethics while prescribing it for anyone else. There is widespread shirking of work and intelligent administrative decisions, by labour and management alike. Efficiency of grievance cells and suggestion boxes is limited by the inefficiency in execution.

Student Stir

The students still have the inertia of pre-independence struggle and speedily identify themselves with the exploited masses and have been up in arms against the usual parental and university authority. Students ape their elders by attempting agitational activities while in school. They are quite certain that for making good as leaders and political somebodies, no grind of education is necessary. They must become leaders of fellow students in almost any agitation that could easily get the youth excited. The blame also rests with teachers who wish to direct the students not by dint of hard work and able leadership in scholarship but by rules and bureaucratic functioning. Learning has been downgraded to just securing good marks in the final examination. Even the semester system has lost all claim to make them work all along and learn problem solving and referral ability. The old examination system depending on large syllabus and lot of choice in the final examination by external examiners is really to be blamed for the low standards in our university and engineering education. Fortunately, there are so many students in India that some brilliant students are always there to confound the onlooker who cannot see how an average student can ever make good in the Indian education system.

How can a teacher or a Vice-Chancellor be opposed to the welfare or success of students? But many students regard them as exploiters. The students blame them for the ills of society. They often see hypocrisy and nepotism even in school administration. In place of preparing for life's work through better skills and training, the students take to agitational skills while in school. One can only suggest that the students must be provided with much more clean and honest environment and the infiltration of politicians among them must be curbed. Students as a class should be assured of maintenance and provided wholesome meals. They can, with some more expense on every individual student, be trained to love simplicity partly by the simple life of community elders whom the school should take pride in bringing closer to the students. Students are sure to react predictably to honest dealings.

Student unions and other student organizations, instead of giving priority to the betterment of education and students' contribution to constructive work, become recruitment agencies for political activists of various political parties. Some of the political student unions are the tails that wag the political party dogs. The Sikh students union was the torch-bearer for the Sikh extremists. They got into this mess by the community permitting political camps in the guise of religious conferences where the student leaders were given cheaply the sense of leadership of the community. The student movement should be channelled afresh into nation-building and planning activities, on the one hand, and purely student interest, on the other. The class and communal interests of the adults in society should not confuse student organizations in a free democratic society. The recent Bidar riot where six Sikh students were killed is an example of misdirected religious education of the Sikhs and the marauding festival cess collectors; both groups had forgotton the true nature of religion, piety and common celebration of festivals.

Migratory Labour

Migratory labour moves from their native villages to possible areas of work expecting good pay and possibility of savings to support their families that stay at home. The workers are untrained usually and can only do manual labour. They build roads, get employment in building civil constructions or as farm labourers. They are unorganized and often get into the clutches of money-lenders and can hardly save much. They rarely have fixed hours of work or any medical cover. Often they have to accept less than the official minimum wage along with deductions for any supplies from the employer like their meals, clothes, etc. Due to calamities also many peasants are reduced to the status of migratory labour. They then form the bulk of the population of pavement dwellers in the big cities or inhabit slums enriching slum landlords and are lorded over by the local bullies.

The welfare state must look after the most deserving cases for welfare of the migratory labour. Most migratory labour is from a pious stock and are thrown to this kind of life only by sheer necessity and lack of proper work in their own localities. Society owes them suitable work to earn their living for which they are willing. Each village or town should have a register of migratory labour and provide them healthy camp life. The employers must be held responsible if there are complaints of cheating and payment of less than the minimum wage. By law the migrant labourer must be paid the full amount earned by him and any return payment for accommodation, meals, loans, etc., should not be deducted and should be settled by the labourer himself. The administration must keep an eye on their welfare since the migratory labour is an important link-pin of an integrated nation.

Bonded Labour

A bonded labourer is almost a slave. The owner of a slave could sell him to serve the master who paid for him. A bonded labourer sells himself for labour so long as savings from the wages do not pay up for the sum taken at start with interest charged on it. The arrangement seems to be mutually beneficial but actually it is an enslaving one. The money taken at the beginning is soon spent on some urgent necessity and the wages are so low, and the employer also charges interest at an exorbitant rate for the initial payment he has made, that the sum with interest can never be paid back during the life-time of the borrower. Sometimes the labour of the wife and children is also claimed by right and the slavery continues from parent to children. The system is in vogue for work for which ordinary labour will not opt, since the conditions of work and hours of work are extremely irksome. Usually brick kilns, shallow-pit mining, lumber business, toddy tapping, household work provide instances of bonded labour. Recently laws have been enacted to free bonded labourers on the basis of legitimate earnings for the work already done for the masters and old debts are to be written off. So far so good. But soon one finds that the freed bonded labourer is starving. He has been trained for nothing but the work he was forced to do and he again seeks the same work at about the same terms. The freeing action would be complete only if the labourer is rehabilitated in some work at normal conditions of employment. It is believed that instructions to the above effect have already been issued to the administrative officials carrying out the court orders to free the bonded labourers. Suitable training for any job and humane treatment is the minimum that society must provide to all adults. The terms for work in irksome conditions must be made humane and amelioration enforced if necessary by nationalizing some major brick kilns, collieries, tanneries, etc.

Workforce of the Government

Government employees are in general better off than ordinary workers in self or private employment. They are assured of housing and medical aid. There is old-age pension and insurance, leave and leave travel concessions, regular working hours, overtime payment, etc. Their grievances are now attended to by separate government departments. The princely governments often auctioned jobs so that they got extra revenue and the officials could squeeze the public. The colonial government did not auction offices but shut its eyes to the illegal gratification and corruption that went on. So much so that the extra illegal income was well recognized and added to the official pay when discussing someone's total emoluments. Such habits of black money income die hard and though officially discouraged, privately they are rampant throughout the line of authority. The extra income now is pooled and distributed right up to the top. The corruption in the high places only trickles down in the form of permissive administration. There is the spectacle of the Posts and Telegraphs employees collecting from house to house *bakshish* on festival days.

Any honest official is dubbed as impractical and not suitable for the requirements of the department. Usually he is shunted from place to place in unimportant jobs requiring least contact with the public since the public must not learn about the possibility of existence of an honest official. The unrest among government servants is only self-created because of competitive ambition and no-holds-barred attitude. Many times the injustice experienced by an official from fellow bureaucrats can be rectified only by appeal to courts or politicians. Any such rectification should also involve punishment of the guilty officials, which at present is not done since they still want to live and let live and everyone can be proved to have skeletons in his cupboard. The work of the departmental grievance cells must be properly monitored since otherwise it might just reduce to being a cosmetic exercise. The government is still the biggest single employer in the country. After first encouraging union activity among the employees in order to catch votes, now the government has discovered how such negative activity has encouraged aggressiveness of the employees and led to inefficiency in work, so much so that the managements refuse to manage lest they tread on some corns. The government has banned union activity in most critical departments and strikes are usually discouraged and declared illegal. Negotiating and welfare machinery is now part of the management. Authorities now claim to be responsible and responsive to all worthwhile suggestions for better conditions of work and better efficiency and production. In principle the workers' training is particularly looked after. Perhaps the Soviet Union needed more openness and reorganization to overcome inefficiency and corruption, we need openness and discipline even if these have to be enforced.

Child Labour

Here is one class which has plenty to complain about. They hardly have means to complain. We have rules in favour of free universal primary education, but children of tender age are seen working in every roadside eating place or in most well-to-do houses or, like Oliver Twist, are hired out almost like bonded labour to all kinds of tyrants. If they escape they become adrift in large cities and enrich literature or movies like Victor Hugo's *gamins* or Rajkapoor's *Awaara*. Many children are supporting their mothers and siblings, being heads of the families. In any dustbin of the city we can see in the early mornings or late at night tender hands of children picking waste paper.

Primarily it is poverty that breaks up families and sends children away to work for their keep. The children who can work but still live with their mothers are counted lucky; most have to stay with acquaintances of their families or in groups with their masters, and soon lose their humanism. Child abuse and knavery or begging falls to their lot. One may agree that some part-time work in order to learn a trade may be necessary for most of the children since, for ages, the trades have been learnt from elders, and it may not be possible to provide free maintenance and high school education to all the children in our country. But whole-time work in sweat shops for little children, be it in carpet weaving or for cotton picking, can be an unredeemed woe. Society should take census of children above the age of four every two years and judge if each child has adequate provision for maintenance and schooling. Those found without adequate means or parental support should be placed in community homes or model children's villages with paid or voluntary adult support. Why should a child first be admitted to an orphanage and only then have claim for better community support. Each inhabited area of about ten thousand souls should boast of at least one children's home where children are taught Indian culture, ethics and a trade. The home can have a small attached farm on which children can learn the art of farming for their own maintenance along with meagre earnings from the handicraft project popular in the area and taught to the children in the home. Constructive workers and voluntary agencies are sure to welcome such a plan with the blessings of private and public sectors. For a healthy society of mature individuals, we have to provide healthy childhood full of acceptance and joy.

Women Workers

From very early times, women have in general been reduced to beasts of burden by the male-dominated society. The weaker sex is reduced to either a decoration piece or to slavery for day and night in the service of her man and family. Certain religions even do not recognize that women have souls. Certain others claim that women's souls also belong to female sex and in every re-birth she will be wife of the same person in different incarnations.

Frugality and stubbornness of women have been deified as *Lakshmi*, the goddess of wealth, and as *Shakti*, the consort of *Siva*, the destroyer. Thus, the only saving grace is that gods must also have their goddesses and men are supposed to honour and respect the women if they hope to have peace and plenty. The mother goddess cult was a major religion of the ancient man. But soon the patriarchal system spread all over the world. Woman was advised to be dependent always and to find fulfilment in serving her man as a god and the family. In India for avoiding crime against women, the practice of marrying them young, burning widows or reducing them to life of denial were started. Women, however, were always assisting in all kinds of labour and handicrafts. Though we do hear about learned women of ancient India or great women soldiers but in general they were not engaged in the professions. In recent times, women's education began in right earnest and now they are recruited for all kinds of work. Discrimination against women is rather veiled. Many regard the higher education of women to be a waste of resources, since the great majority of highly educated women squander their ability in minor jobs in order to look after their families. In fact, the life of an educated working woman is doubly as hard as that of a working man. After doing the day's work in an office or factory she has to have no respite from daily chores of cooking and mending. When the children are just arriving or are very small, in general in India because baby-sitting services are still elementary, many housewives give up jobs even if they had held on to them earlier. Later, after a few years, when the children can somehow do without the mother's continuous attendance, she has been so much out of touch with her job that many find excuses like the husband's earning is sufficient so that they no longer wish to go back to work. For a woman, even just going to work in a municipal bus is an ordeal. Even in the office only now they are trying to provide some facilities for women employees to relax. The best way is for each office or factory to have a small quota of jobs split up as part-time ones for women with small children living in nearby localities if they are suitably qualified and are interested. This concession to young mothers should not be regarded as partiality based on sex. Thus, the superior training of most women will not be wasted since very soon the part-time women workers will move to full-time jobs especially because they would never be cut off from their work. The part-time employee mothers should be retired from their part-time jobs in five years or at about the age of thirty when they should be in a position to enter permanent employment.

It can easily be verified that women labourers, for full and equal day-long work, are paid less than what is paid to men. This discrimination is illegal. Future of women workers is certainly going to be bright. They have already made their mark in the professions:

teaching, medicine, law, administration, banking, etc. In studies they are doing as well as or generally better than the men. In India the number of academic awards won by girl students in universities or the IITs is proportionally much larger than by the boys.

Society must also have a close look at the status of housewives. They work practically full-time and are on call each and every day for 24 hours of the day with no leave. We do not visualize that things will ever come to a head when housewives will ask for unionization and service agreements from the head of any family. The whole concept of family is for each to serve to the best of his ability and to accept what is allotted to him or her. But to neglect woman who has slogged for her whole life for the family in her old age, especially if she happens to become a widow, and leave her at the mercy of the daughers-in-law is unjust. The device that will give solace to housewives is to declare that they are also an important segment of self-employed workers. They should be allowed to show a minimum notional if not actual income from their housewife function in their tax returns being the estimated economic return for managing their small families. Since they are surrendering the entire notional income to the family a small amount should be set apart by society as old-age pension or insurance for the housewife. Where workers are entitled to unemployment relief, the housewives should be entitled to old-age relief, or old-age insurance from community contributions or contributions from loving husbands and families when the women are active as housewives.

Democracy and evolutionary development of mankind to *ahimsa* from violence, to knowledge from ignorance, to modernization from drudgery and superstition and to small families from large ones will go a long way towards the emancipation of women without any violent conflict based on sex.

Unemployment

Continuous unemployment will cause frustration for any worker and can make him a willing recruit for agitations, violence and all kinds of conflicts. Mahatma Gandhi had declared:

> "I shall work for an India in which the poorest shall feel that it is their country in whose making they have an effective voice, an India in which there shall be no high class or low class of people, in which all communities shall be in perfect harmony . . . in which the

interest of the dumb millions will be scrupulously respected."

The first priority is to provide the basic necessities of food, clothing and shelter to all. The only way to assure this in an economy of scarcity is to provide work for all. We support the move that right to work be regarded also as a fundamental right and growing poverty must be reversed. Resources must be created to give an unemployment dole to anyone who cannot be provided work according to his ability. Revolutionary steps have been taken to alleviate poverty by the government spending on the 20-point programme, but government itself states that only 20 per cent of the funds actually reach the target population, the rest being absorbed by the distribution channel mainly by the political hangers-on and the bankers and the contractors. The moral is that the government's house-keeping needs a thorough shake-up in their methods of selecting their bureaucracy and agents. A better way might be to openly spend the money through non-political constructive work cells spread throughout the country from the times and labours of leaders of the Gandhian movement. The nationalized banks in their scheme of loans for generating self-employment have done a great service for generating employment, but a thorough monitoring of this activity has become necessary as the statistics of loans given is less important than the monthly income of the borrower and of the bank as a result of a loan over successive periods. Squandering of the loan money in a few months will not take the nation far. The political parties would do well to have active workers or cadres who can assist in the planning and monitoring of the nation-building activities to gain the confidence of the people. Only such political parties be allowed to function in this activity which believe in the correctness of both ends and means. Unethical short cuts and calumnies will not build our nation whether we have laws curbing character assassination or not. The entire technical manpower could be relatively easily harnessed to education, sanitation and recycling of materials. An agricultural country like India should produce enough so as to spare for exports. There is so much emphasis on the biggest energy resource of India, viz. the solar energy and the most efficient use of solar energy is in agriculture, growth of forests and of fodder. It is the excess of agricultural production which eventually will finance all industrial and service projects. We have a large population, but each person is endowed with hands and brain. If the people are trained in some productive pursuit and energy is available, all kinds of work can be carried out for production, or for service to the people. Education and training can easily absorb about 10 per cent of our entire workforce. Education and training is the key to increased employment or to larger incomes and we can neglect proper education and training only at the cost of survival of our country.

The moment we have an agitation, misguided students and unemployed youth join in and are dragged into anti-social activities and violence by the example of criminal elements to whom the riots are godsent opportunity for may' .m and plunder. It would perhaps be in order to have proper selection and training even of the active workers of any political party so that the riff-raff cannot masquerade as them. The mass political parties should have ward committees at the grassroots level. They can also look after the anti-poverty and environmental and conservation programmes including monitoring of the government programmes. Preferably the ward committees should be representative of the entire population of the ward and there should be constructive workers from all political parties in these as some kind of voluntary *panchayats*. Such committees will have duties as well as finances and popular authority to raise funds by levies of cash and kind.

4

INTERNATIONAL CO-EXISTENCE

Introduction

WE USE the word 'co-existence' meaning tolerance for various religions, communities, ideologies and classes within India. The principle of co-cxistence actually came into currency from international affairs meaning live and let live philosophy for nations. Nehru and Chou En-lei enunciated the *Panch Sheel* principles of co-existence in international affairs primarily for sorting out the differences among neighbouring nations like India and China. The non-aligned group of nations also believes in the futility of military alliances and in the possible co-existence of opposing ideologies, like free enterprise and socialism. The alternative to co-existence in international affairs is war or preparation for war. Nations should concentrate on the elimination of hostility and not on elimination of hostile countries. Peaceful co-existence could then develop into mutually beneficial international co-operation.

Historical Background

Hostility and war are opposite to co-existence. Western nations in the history of the world have believed in the hostility of others or friendship only in pacts against some common enemies. It is the preoccupation with hostility that led some countries during a war to demand unconditional surrender of the enemy. Such was the demand of the allies just before their victory and such was almost the demand of Khomeini just before the negotiated cease-fire in the Iran-Iraq war. Israel justifies its intransigent attitude about the Palestinian State by claiming that the Arabs will never accept the existence of Israel.

Pakistani dictatorship believed that India was permanently hostile to her since India, in their belief, had never reconciled to the partition when it actually took place on a secular and democratic basis (riots took place on communal basis only at the instigation of communalists). Communist dogma insists that according to their god of historical necessity and its prophet, Marx, communism must replace capitalism. The peace-makers say that pessimistic forebodings must be buried and co-existence will bring mutual friendship leading to co-operation and finally to a universal diversified culture enriching the life of every nation. Already India is experimenting with the socialistic pattern of society giving an honoured place to both capitalism and socialism in the service of the people and their welfare. The communist countries are bidding good-bye to communes and trusting the private profit motive in many subtle ways in the interest of increased efficiency and production.

The vision of Woodrow Wilson resulted in the establishment of the League of Nations being the first forum to discuss peace and war and to bolster international co-operation. The welfare of the ceded territories was enjoined, with the goal of eventual freedom of the subject people from the mandatory powers. Labour problems and problems of emigration and world meteorology, etc., were handled. The League was wrecked by the emergence of fascist states believing in the adage of "might is right" and the self-seeking of all nations who could have done but did not effectively intervene in the rape of Ethiopia and the toppling of the democratic state in Spain, or in the Soviet attack on Finland.

After the Second World War the United Nations was established to salvage internationalism from the growing power of the nation states and utter involvement in nationalism of the people of the colonial empires of the allies. The emergence of superpowers and attempt of smaller powers to attain strength by alignment with one superpower or the other caused the emergence of armed camps. The United Nations was practically made ineffective in curbing superpowers and in blocking jealousies and proxy wars. The invention of the nuclear bomb and sophisticated weapons aggravated the threat of mutual destruction. The voice of reason and the emergence of free India through non-violence gave a new lease to the hope of international peace and solution of international conflicts by peaceful means. This has brought a new focus of attention on the United Nations as the forum, where all nations have equal say and, within the constraint of original functioning of veto, etc., bring about negotiated termination of hostilities. Co-existence implies peace including the positive relationship of tolerance, justice, equality and goodwill.

The diplomatic activity, the policy of peace and openness in international affairs is very recent. Very few countries ever sought peace with their neighbours as equals. There was distrust of all foreign countries. The doctrine of balance of power and of military alliances with secret clauses prevailed. Wars were almost continuous with some intervals of peace. Often the wars were the result of jealousy and fear and each side believed in opportunistic as well as pre-emptive fights. The philosophy of co-existence implies self-reliance and places trust on the conscience of the entire humanity. No country possessing only conventional weapons can stand in battle up to a country armed with nuclear weapons, unless it can count on the support of all mankind including the people of the nuclear bomb-owning country against the use of such weapons. The primary thrust for peace and co-existence has come from the Third World countries and from some developed countries who also joined the non-aligned movement from a realistic appreciation of the dangers from reliance on nuclear weapons and military support of one or the other nuclear power. Most people now understand the dead-end of mutual distrust and wastage of rare resources of men and materials in warlike preparations when the alternative of plenty to share through mutual co-operation and new technical advance is there. The decision of the USA and the Soviet Union at the Soviet initiative to methodically and progressively destroy all nuclear weapons in order eventually to have a nuclear-free world and to de-escalate tensions in recognized trouble spots like Afghanistan, Kampuchea, Nicaragua, Middle East, etc., must be regarded as the beginning of the co-existence era in world affairs. Nearer home the moment a democratic government in Pakistan starts trusting Indian vows regarding co-existence, there will be both international and internal peace in both the countries.

We have seen how an international conflict spreads and engulfs one country after another. Peace also spreads from one region to another. The current stance of co-existence among the superpowers has helped quieten troubled conditions in many parts of the world. There is another logical evolution in world affairs. Regional groupings are growing in strength. This is a step towards eventual world government. The stage was set by inter-American co-operation under the hegemonistic influence of the United States and the establishment of the European Economic Co-operation under the threat of the Soviet bloc, but apart from these unions shedding colonial and defensive origins, there are new regional bodies obviously for mutual benefit and for the stability of the entire world, like the Asean, the Organization of African Unity and the beginnings of the SAARC. Mutual suspicions in South Asia will be smothered by the climate of co-operation generated by the South Asian Association for Regional Co-operation. Now that Iran-Iraq conflict has ended, there is hope that western Asia will also have its regional body once the Palestinian issue is resolved through negotiation. The democratic rights of the majority population of a country must first be restored before a nation can really contribute to world peace. The minority governments or dictators will have only one principle, that of self-preservation, and no other commitment to freedom, equality or progress. The current gulf crisis is being vigorously handled by the United Nations.

War and Peace

War is essentially a result of overcrowding. When the primitive men hunted and found competition from other tribal groups, they resorted to fighting, accusing each other of trespassing into their customary hunting grounds. Whenever a State or a kingdom felt the crunch of resources and an overflowing or empty treasury, it resorted to aggression and expansion. It was much later that expansion was also tied to the visions of one world under a single authority like that of Alexander, Chengiz Khan or Napoleon. Overcrowding in England together with the industrial revolution in Europe consolidated the empires of England, France and Holland. Spanish colonial empire had grown in the new world because of bold ventures of Iberian sailors. European fears bred the empires of Hitler, Mussolini and Stalin. The American and the communist hegemonies have only now lost their expansionist edge. Most empires enslaved or squandered the resources of the world for the benefit of the few, and also set up many petty dictators in emulation of the mighty ones.

In parallel to wars of conquest, many wars have been waged to keep the enslaved people down. The fight in the Congo, or in Vietnam, was such a war. Wars of ideology have been rare, the only true example being the civil wars in China or in Spain. Ideologies prefer to conquer peacefully with perhaps a last resort to arms as the expansion of the Caliph's Islamic empire. World history is full of expansionist wars imposed by ambitious nations or monarchs like Hans of China, Czars of Russia, rulers of Germany, France, Sweden (during early 18th century), Ranjit Singh of the Punjab, etc. The perfect example of an expansionist country throughout its history has been the Persian kingdoms. Allied with the Arabs, the Persians destroyed the old Central Asian city States. From that destruction these could never recover. The Muslims of Central Asia opted for the Czar and the communists in preference to Persian ministrations. Crusades could also be classified under wars of ideology, but these were like adolescent attempts at heroics. Many wars when denuded of wrappings of patriotism and heroics were only opportunistic or pre-emptive. The Japanese were supposed to have struck at Pearl Harbour in an opportunistic move and dropping of the atom bombs on Japan is supposed to be pre-emptive against their continued resistance. Hitler's attack on Russia was pre-emptive with a calculation that Japan will continue to threaten Russia's eastern flank. Iran-Iraq war was the culmination of ancient hatreds aggravated by the arms suppliers of the 20th century.

Most wars only partially satisfied the victors and brought misery on the victor and the vanquished alike. The actual history has a single track and it is difficult to substantiate what would have happened but for certain accidental twists of fortune. On summation of war and peace aims of any belligerents, the sum total of achievement of any war is negative, but for some advances in the sciences and technologies on account of war-time pressures and later their applications to peaceful uses. But this cannot make up for the widespread misery, crowds of refugees, destruction of resources, political upheavals and churning up of society. The conflicts rarely get resolved or sublimated, these only get smothered in a euphoria of victory or hopelessness of defeat and arise phoenix like unless the two sets of politicians have an enlightened approach in favour of peace and co-existence. Perhaps in the adolescent period of mankind now about to end, wars were the governess aiding evolution of human civilization.

Wars, however, are not biologically inevitable. Hardly any creature other than man kills another of the same species. The man's nature as human being is humanism and *ahimsa*. He should improve his environment only through *ahimsa*, though he is expected to defend it even by violence, since abject surrender is against his grain. Mahatma Gandhi felt that man could defend his values best by non-violence (of the brave). As Radhakrishnan observed:

Human civilization should be judged by the peaks in culture at any period, the human qualities are essentially in the appreciation of love and truth as proclaimed by all great men of the world. The true flowering of the human nature will occur when everyone is assured of his right to his essential requirements and he has his freedoms and equality of opportunity.

This might be possible in the near future because of the realization of the finite nature of many resources and the attempts to stabilize the world population as well as from the advances in science and technology that might assure mankind very soon of unlimited energy and clever recycling of materials as well as invention of efficient tailored materials. If the drudgery is removed from work, who will want to be dubbed an aggressor or attempt to enslave others. In the new era, the floods and droughts would be controlled and the climate made friendly. With open invitation and opportunities to travel and to visit others, there would be no need to wage wars. The new weapons of war make it necessary that war is outlawed and the criminals who attempt to spring a war must be tried as criminals and punished by an international peace-keeping force, as the Indian peace-keeping Force did to the militants in Sri Lanka out to create a dictatorship of a coterie of militants in the Tamil majority areas of Sri Lanka. It is time that a world peace-keeping force is deployed at various centres under the auspices of a world body. In the past, most peace treaties had secret clauses that unabashedly meant preparation for the next war. The refreshing new policy of openness and emphasis on *ahimsa* by some of the spokesmen of the nations are the confrontation of the good in man against the evil that stands unmasked.

Security

Security in freedom is necessary for each nation to develop according to its genius. Unilateral disbandment of its army will not give it security even from the internal trouble-makers, nor can it have security by means of non-aggression pacts or guarantees from powerful countries. The examples of Russian-German non-aggression pact and the failure of guarantees to Poland or Finland are ever fresh in people's memory. The big powers only play a game of offering security and then making the offer conditional and withdrawing the protection at the critical moment. Militarily weak countries are used only as pawns and not as allies. The only way to win security is not by having a deterrent collection of atom bombs since the protection offered by these bombs is of sure destruction even in the so-called victory. No nation can afford to provide a nuclear umbrella to others if it exposes itself to a nuclear attack. Deterrent punishment also would not cancel a crime already perpetrated. Just as nations are free from internal threats because of their investment in police and armed forces for the enforcement of the rule of law, in the same way there must be an international law and an international law enforcement agency for the security of the entire world. So long as we do not have a democratic world government, we must strengthen the Security Council of the United Nations by placing all weapons wherever manufactured and wherever stocked under the control and jurisdiction of the U.N. Security Council. There will have to be some structural changes like the overruling of the veto by 80 per cent vote of the General Assembly. The United Nations could have some directly controlled police and commando forces to combat terrorism and *coup d'etat* against the Secretary General and to assure its safe working even from randomly chosen sites. The prohibition against chemical weapons has been repeatedly flouted and same may happen if the nuclear weapons are only forbidden unless there is an international control of all such weapons and their use.

International Law

Once we accept the possibility of an international security enforcement system, the availability of international justice and its binding jurisdiction on the entire world becomes necessary. A system of justice through appropriate juries could be envisaged. The jury could be chosen with one member each from the geographical region of the litigants, the other two should be from the regions with which the concerned litigants have most trade. These four regional members of the jury must be from those who had at one time or the other held important positions connected with the U.N. system. The appeal against the decision based on jury verdict will only be to the Security Council itself.

Codification of international law especially in matters already coming under the purview of the United Nations agencies must begin and be based on consensus, with the compulsory adherence of all nations. Provisions for adjudication and reconciliation must also exist prior to the recourse to judicial verdict which will always be enforced. Observing the recent successful efforts of the Secretary General in assisting negotiations and talks for peace, his hands can be strengthened by having a permanent conciliation commission directly responsible to the Secretary General and reporting its success or failure to the Security Council. The disputants could directly ask the Secretary General for help in reconciliation. When the Security Council declares any disputed area in the world as a hot spot, for example, it may deem it necessary one day to declare the West Bank of Jordan or even South Africa or Afghanistan a hot spot then the area will have to be occupied and governed directly by the United Nations for five years in the first instance or till it can be suitably and safely made self-governing according to democratic wishes of the people of that area. Such areas under the temporary rule of the United Nations will also be temporarily the garrison stations for the United Nations forces. Such steps can bring global security and peace to the world which is now at the threshold of a great new jump into a future of peace and plenty.

United Nations

The establishment of the United Nations in 1946 was a momentous step for the co-existence of nations. It was a giant step for mankind indeed. Setting up of the United Nations also accelerated the growth of regional groupings aspiring for regional co-operation within the U.N. system. The resolutions of the United Nations so far are only recommendations and their acceptance by a particular nation is only voluntary since everyone wants to preserve his national sovereignty. The regional associations bring the members closer and the agreed decisions are quickly put into practice. The snag in the regional groupings is mainly financial since financial contribution still is voluntary and has no proportion fixed for the worth of a project, and the ability to pay of a member. Where the projects can earn revenue, the finances could be had from international banking on commercial terms.

Main initiatives for peace have often come from the less strong non-aligned nations. These countries are also agitating for a new economic order and new information system. A simple first step is to have U.N. television and radio broadcasts available in every corner of the world. This will be second giant step in the forward march of the nations to the desired new information system and to world peace.

The Universal Declaration of Human Rights includes:

Article I

All human beings are born free and equal in dignity and rights. They are endowed with reason and conscience and should act towards one another in a spirit of brotherhood.

Article II

Everyone is entitled to all the rights and freedoms set forth in the declaration without distinction of any kind such as race, colour, sex, language, religion, political and other opinions, national or social origin, property, birth or other status.

The United Nations has many other active international agencies like the International Labour Organization, the World Bank, the Food and Agriculture Organization, the World Health Organization, the International Council of Scientific Unions and many Inter-governmental organizations for specific tasks often under the umbrella of the United Nations Educational, Scientific and Cultural Organization (UNESCO) or other U.N. agencies.

World organizations have developed quickly in areas where common interests of all nations are involved, e.g. in health, food, communications, etc. The world bodies have to work through consensus since action is still with sovereign nation states. The Law of the Sea Treaty though arrived at by consensus is still not signed by four developed nations. International organizations should have working channels of direct communication with concerned agencies in any national State so that the national action on various proposals and recommendations is quicker. Perhaps the U.N. radio and television networks when set up will facilitate direct and quick communications. We are close to the times of world culture, of unity in diversity, of secularism and co-existence based on trust and mutual respect transcending all conflicts.

International Co-operation

There is an urgent need for the rich and the poor nations to come together in their common understanding of the goals of full employment and further development everywhere. Willy Brandt's Independent Commission has recommended the emergence of an advisory body for the monitoring of all development activities of the U.N. Already, on the recommendation of the General Assembly expert group, a Director General of Development and International Economic Co-operation has been appointed. There would be increasing contribution from the developing countries to the processing, marketing and distribution of commodities. There is need of elimination of certain tariffs against processed commodities and the establishment of fair and equitable international transport rates. The mutual interest of producing and consuming countries in the development of mineral resources requires the creation of new financial arrangements leading to more equitable and stable mineral development arrangements. Industrialization of developing countries will provide increasing opportunity for world trade. It should be facilitated as a matter of international policy. The overall management of the world monetary system should have the participation of the whole world community. Willy Brandt has felt the need for the establishment of a World Development Fund having recourse to universal and automatic funding "The dynamism of the newly industrialized countries can be accommodated in a more expansionary phase of the world economy."

5

CENTRE-STATE RELATIONS AND INTER-STATE DISCORDS

Introduction

THE INTER-STATE problems regarding border regions and religious or linguistic minorities will not be addressed here since these have already been covered. The major inter-State discords have arisen because of disputes regarding sharing of river water resources or related to inter-State trading. Usually the inter-State discords and Centre-State issues do not get adverse publicity if the political party, controlling the two States or the Centre and the State in question, is the same. Then the disputes get swept under the carpet for the common political authorities at the top to sort out at their convenience. But when the political parties controlling the disputants are different, the issues are often inflated beyond reason and vociferous bickering results often leading to serious erosion of the single family or co-operative federation ideal. Very often the Centre-State quarrels are the result of political party ambitions with regard to scoring of points against the other party for winning the next elections. The Governor, who is an appointee of the Centre, has to ensure smooth working of the State Government in the national interest sometimes held synonymous with the posture of the political party controlling the Central government. There is also the requirement of the Governor functioning in State matters within the wishes of the elected chief minister belonging to a political party which may be in the opposition at the Centre. The Governor in such a dual responsibility situation has to win the confidence of both the Centre and the State and much will depend on healthy conventions and the personalities of the various incumbents.

Certain States condone or legalize discrimination in favour of locals in the matter of work and employment and there are also Central directions to discriminate in favour of certain backward tribes and classes. Though the provisions were introduced as temporary in nature, yet later these have been extended in time as well as in sweep with a vengeance and in many states there have been violent agitations against the scope of such provisions as creating conditions crystallizing fissiparous distinctions when the urgent need is to create an equal citizenship of the country. This problem has also been briefly touched upon earlier. The desired results can be realized through intelligent administrative measures without harming the equality-of-opportunity issue. All jobs can be suitably described including, among desirable qualifications, the knowledge of local language or sociological tests favouring certain backward patterns of life. The criterion for selection should be uniform for all Indian citizens.

In this chapter the main consideration will be given to economic and fiscal problems that often give rise to disputes between governments of State or the Centre. The development and planning activity of one State naturally has an impact, environmental as well as economic, on other States. The inter-State co-operation and removal of such difficulties must be dealt with at as low a level as possible. The inter-State discussions should precede involvement of the Centre as a referee or even as an arbitrator. A joint family or enterprise is impossible if there is not a recognized authority for arbitration which has to be obeyed in the larger interest of the whole. There are also well-known opportunities for inter-State assistance in the times of natural calamities and shortages in any State compared to the relatively better-off neighbours in that respect. Immediate assistance becomes necessary at the time of famine, drought, floods, earthquakes, riots, etc. There must be built-in conventions for inter-State initiatives without the Centre's involvement. Centre-State relations can be healthy if it is realized that India is not just a federation of States but is rather a unitary State or at least a co-operative federation.

Planning Process

The easy way is only to look at the projects started and expense incurred during a year and then keep adding a small amount of about 5 per cent of the expenditure during the previous year at fixed prices. When certain projects get completed or start producing wealth, or new financial resources have been made available, some genuine planning efforts must be made. The selected project should be important for the society as assured by pre-determined priorities and the project should be feasible. There are well-known quantitative methods comparing the social importance of the competing projects. The whims and predilections of politicians and pressure groups should not alone sway the decision. The priority goals in the present situation are of employment and production. The planners must guard against the completed project becoming a white elephant. One must guard against gigantism and permissive planning that allows projects to remain non-profitable after the stage of experimental production. Employment generation irrespective of contribution to more profits and production must have no place in our planning. Of course the build-up of the infrastructure and of services, entertainment, dissemination of information, national health, education, etc., have their own place in planning for which productive projects have to create wealth along with borrowings and development grants from friendly countries and financial institutions. Similarly national development would be impossible if there is not the tranquillity through internal and external security and highest priority is not given to the eradication of poverty and to provision of right to work for all. This will happen if the production of goods and services most widely required are on the priority project lists and the planning is not limited to requirements of the richer luxury-oriented classes, which could be met by limited imports.

The feasibility of a project is extremely important. A project must be thoroughly analysed in all its aspecto; the availability of infrastructure, the timely completion of preliminary activities and the completion with achieving of results within a reasonable planned period (usually not exceeding few years). Public loses interest in projects that keep going on and on without concrete results for a long time. Evidently in such cases the pursuit of development was insincere and purposeless or checks were not maintained. The site of a project must be decided on scientific principles and objectivity. The selected site must be spacious permitting future expansion and be such as can conveniently attract raw materials as well as skilled and trained manpower. In Indian conditions, preference also works for backward areas so that more work opportunities are provided to the neglected segments of the Indian society. In the pursuit of the social goals, infrastructure must be developed first in our backward states so that there is true equality of opportunity in our country. Programme

Evaluation and Review Technique (PERT) and CPM (Critical Path Method) project planning and management techniques are of great help. The control and evaluation organization should be separate from the executing organization.

There have been complaints from States that the Central Planning Commission has been sometimes usurping the functions of the State or the Central Cabinet. If there is any truth in such complaints, necessary correction must be made. The planning body has got to stay as an advisory body. It must have the necessary political inputs from all levels in the political parties as well as the Central and State Governments. But the Planning Commission is primarily a body of scientific experts including economists, lawyers and finance wizards from banking and industry, besides advisers on emerging technologies, material and energy resources as well as consultants on health, geography, environment, education, etc. Planning cells must exist in State ministries and at district levels. The monitoring organization should be part of the statistical or information set-up at each district, State or Central ministry level. Ideally, the planning methodology must develop and spread from the Centre but the detailed plans must be integrated as these are first outlined at lower levels. During the overall plan integration, the question of competing sites, relative priorities and migration of workers can be dealt with. Many times independent planning of projects unnecessarily increases recruitment of practically superfluous staff. As far as possible new projects must be placed in existing ministries, industries and organizations so that staff already existing for low activity or completed projects can be diverted to new work. One of the factors influencing the geographic location should be the possible agreed diversion of existing staff to it by the State concerned on deputation/transfer to the project. The differences between the planners, executives and the monitors must be sorted out in an objective manner. The inter-State and the Centre-State conflicts in planning matters should be adjudicated by small judicial committees composed of wise and respected people from any walk of life who can devote time to this necessary task. Depending on past experience, conventions can be built for dealing with policies and expenditure for the subjects on the Concurrent List between the Centre and the States. The National Development Council should be a forum where the States can present their case through their technical experts. The proceedings of the National Development Council should be made public so that the public can understand if there is divergence between the popular view as reflected in the decision and the technical view as clarified in the discussions. The chairman should normally be accepted as the arbitrator for individual projects when there is no decision possible by consensus after the views of the experts have been considered. The public hearings of the National Development Council will educate all concerned in project decisions and smother the unseemly controversies about discrimination against certain States. The discrimination cannot be ignored when we actually see many States blessed by all the bounties of nature and with a history of excellence of human materials, but now dismally poor.

There should be a clear policy of allocation of financial resources to the States. The allocation should be such as will not require too many *ad hoc* revisions and *ad hoc* grants to certain States. Additional grants could be made on the basis of performance and on showing better performance. The running expenditure on ongoing projects, schemes, security, education and health should possibly be limited to about 50 per cent of the available resources and 50 per cent of the total resources, savings, share of taxes, loans and grants be earmarked for new projects to be started that year or to be carried forward from previous years if the project has not yet begun giving the desired results. In case an old project does not show the expected results in about three years, it must be materially modified or preferably scrapped and responsibility of mis-planning, mis-execution or laxity in monitoring pin-pointed. Planned development includes also new projects dealing with infrastructure, communications, administration, health, education, etc.

States like Jammu & Kashmir and Assam which have institutionalized discrimination in favour of State citizens should preferably dismantle such apartheid or at least take a commonsense decision in favour of a quota of immigrants from other States on the basis of existing data about emigration of own State citizens to other States for seasonal or permanent jobs. Such quotas will help the integration of the country and be beneficial to all States without the States losing any of their special status.

Inter-State Problems

River Water Disputes

Such inter-State or international disputes arise because rivers flow from one State (country) to another. In general, incoming water is welcome for supplies of drinking water, for irrigation or industrial use or for flushing of waterways and often the complaint is that the sending State takes away disproportionate amount releasing only a smaller share for the receiving State. When the incoming water causes floods, or too much waterlogging and salination of soil or deposit of unproductive silt and sand, the complaint is that the sending State should have controlled the release and allowed only limited amount to the downstream State. The natural solution is the co-operative use of the river waters with recognition of mutual rights and requirements. There is the necessity of building reservoirs for flood control, hydro-electric projects and irrigation canal systems in all reaches of the river to the extent technically and economically feasible. For alleviation of floods, besides building storage reservoirs along the river flow, there is urgent necessity for building small innumerable tanks in the plains to control rainwater and to provide water resource for pisciculture and recreation parks for all sizes of habitations. Floods are often augmented dangerously by rains in the plains and not necessarily by the rains in the source region of the river. Indian plains have been dotted with a large number of tanks in the past, but with the advent of piped water supplies, neighbourhood tanks have now lost significance and their role in flood control forgotten. Large reservoirs and multi-purpose river valley projects need lot of finance. India and Pakistan could solve their Indus basin water-sharing problems through the good offices of the United Nations and the World Bank. Discussion and arbitration are the only means for resolving all disputes. For inter-State problems the good offices of the National Development Council through expert commissions should be relatively easy. There is also a statutory provision for setting up of tribunals under the Inter-State Water Dispute Act, only the action has to be expedited or ensured through an amendment to the Act as suggested by the Sarkaria Commission.

Environment

Indians have had a tradition of ritualistic cleanliness, but were not very careful about the co-operative effort necessary for a clean environment. There is not much cleanliness if one area is kept meticulously clean but the refuse is scattered in a neighbouring area. Or one class of people create a clean micro-environment for individuals of their class at the cost of utter degradation of individuals belonging to another class. Cleanliness has to be systematic and the whole environment must be society's affair. Pollution must not spread to the rivers and to the atmosphere. Water currents and wind will pollute distant areas if pollutants are indifferently discharged upstream. We must be thankful that India realized, though late, that the river Ganges, held holy by millions, was becoming polluted. The cleaning of the Ganges has begun in right earnest with the help of the international community.

Disaster overtakes an area where the green cover suffers excessive destruction. Foothills of the Himalayas and the hills of Maharashtra have lost this cover and there is loss of the soil through erosion. The bleak hills cannot hold rainwater causing many springs to dry resulting in irrigation loss. Every State is now making earnest efforts to plant trees and create man-made forests as well as husband the forest wealth scientifically. The forest management should not be held up at the State borders but forests should be treated as the nation's wealth entrusted to various States for local management. Forest management is the first step also for river management.

No one wants stronger nations to ignore the interests of weaker nations or island communities when getting rid of nuclear wastes or carrying out nuclear explosions, similarly within our country every effort has to be made to fully containerize and localize the nuclear wastes from our nuclear power plants till we can master the technology of obtaining power from nuclear fusion which is pollution free. Control of stack gases, smoke, locust flights across State borders has to be exercised even if industries may have to he pushed back towards the interior and the effluents purified. Cooperative spraying of locust-breeding grounds becomes necessary.

Control of pollution might lead to co-operation for control of human pollutants like the terrorists and smugglers. Strengthening of the intelligence departments and cultivation of friendly feelings and intercourse are the necessary anti-pollution measures in these matters. Zonal councils could be formed for inter-State co-operation in controlling pollution and disturbances before asking the Centre to intervene.

Fiscal Measures

In general, if the produce of one State is mainly processed and value added in another State, market conditions should normally determine the price of the basic raw material or the commodity. The State and the Centre usually charge an excise duty over the processed produce or the finished goods. The State providing the major raw material or energy resource should be given a share of the excise duty for its own development. There must not be exploitation of a raw material producing State within the country. Mineral resources of Bihar and Orissa have enriched in the recent past other States and other countries but not these poor States. The oil-producing States in the country including the States with off-shore resources are entitled to a share of the national profits being made on their crude. Similar considerations should prevail in the case of production of power by the Centre from the hydro-electric potential existing in a particular State. Most of the problems concerning sharing of power could be solved by giving a legitimate right over the profits to the State where the resource has been located. Same principle must be worked out for export of sugarcane or other agricultural crops to food-processing and sugar-producing factories in other States. The primary producer must not be left at the mercy of bounties from others but should have certain rights over the profits likely to be made by the added value from factory processing. The economists can work out such shares proportionate to resources put in by the primary producing States.

Trade and Commerce

Inter-State problems arise when the traders in one State have complaints about the hurdles placed by another State in the free flow of trade and commerce. Such issues can arise about all kinds of items of trade and commerce and must be thoroughly examined by a standing panel of experts from the two States so that a reasonable free flow of trade can continue which is the aim of a co-operative federation.

Centre-State Problems

Sharing of Revenues

Many commissions and committees have considered how to share the revenues collected by the Centre between the Centre and the States. First, every effort should be made to fully collect the taxes that are due and States have considerable responsibility to assist the Centre so that it has more funds to share. Every levy must have a laid down proportion which reverts to each State. As discussed earlier, certain States will have greater share based on their contribution to the raw materials and other inputs. The remaining general share of the States has to be distributed on the basis of their needs and reduced if they have shown indifference or inefficiency in efforts towards the national planning goals. Any project must first be proposed by a State through its own planners and technologists and ardently desired by their negotiating politicians and then accepted by the National Development Council without being hustled by agitational tactics. Thus, a State must do its home-work before it can receive its share of the Central funds. For raising more avenues of income, the Sarkaria Commission suggests further consideration to taxing the agricultural income, raising the monetary limit of Rs. 250 p.a. of professional, etc., tax and making corporation tax as permissibly shareable. Also Central cesses if levied must be for a specific purpose and for a limited period. The subject of taxation of 'Advertisement broadcast by radio or television' should also be included in media advertisement. The system of tax-free municipal bonds should be introduced. Free foreign exchange to the extent of a small fraction of a State's annual budget should be placed at its disposal. There should be constant review of the Centre-State sharing of revenues by the Finance Commission. These and other Sarkaria Commission observations can smoothen the relations still further. The populist measures by States must not be at the cost of progress of development work. State Planning and Finance Boards should be set up with an eye on proper distribution of resources and projects to cover various regions of the State. The revision of royalty rates for petroleum and natural gas should be made every two years. Less-developed States should get more revenue transfers. The issue of shares, licences, bonds, etc., should be decentralized so that there is no difficulty for residents of remote and backward areas. Most of these steps can be taken up without the need to amend the Constitution.

Concurrent List

The complementary and supplementary roles of the States and the Centre must be further explained by discussions on the subjects on the Concurrent List. If the States are to spread education, let the Centre look after the laying down of the standards and the national priorities in education. The Centre should set up organizations that can produce trained teachers and educationists, preachers and instructors in secular morality and sports. The British Council is doing well in many such spheres in the countries of the Commonwealth and the Centre can emulate such efforts for the States. The Centre must develop at least a link language for science, a language with a suitable script and vocabulary for science and technology which can be understood with minimum effort by Indians of all States – both urban and rural. The continued use of English as the language of the sciences, engineering and medicine will create an unbridgeable gulf between the city and the village folks that may lead us to an internal disastrous upheaval.

While the States run the country's routine health services, the Centre must help them have prestigious research in medicine and in medical technology. The Centre has also a concurrent responsibility to make available cheaper medicines, medical instruments and to encourage parallel if not integrated practice of Allopathy, Ayurveda, Unani and Homeopathic systems of medicine. Medical science is fast developing. Already a practising doctor has spent more time in his college education than any other young engineer or scientist. All medical education should be a charge on the Centre and admissions only on merit must be permitted at every entry point into medical education or medical services career. For the development of the infrastructure in the States, the Central planning and reservoir of resources and administration must have a respectable role. According to the Sarkaria Commission, the residuary powers of legislation in regard to taxation should be placed on the Concurrent List. The inter-governmental council visualized in the Constitution should be set up to sort out snags, if any, in the working of the Concurrent List. Railway, Union and such other properties should also be liable to taxes like any other property for similar use.

States' Rights

States have their specific rights in a co-operative federation which is the Union of India. In many areas they can formulate their own laws and rules. In the Concurrent List they have independence in the execution of their plans and in the use of resources allowed from the Central reservoir. The Sarkaria Commission has lately gone into some of the complaints but have not come up with any really novel ideas. There are universal problems of unemployment, inefficiency, maladministration, delay in providing justice, moral vacuum, etc. Let the States show initiative in dealing with such pressing problems outside the beaten track and if they find hurdles because of interference of the Central authority through armed forces and courts or financial policies there would be time enough to study a more loose political system in the interest of the welfare of the common man. An inter-State council would resolve any controversial issues between States or between the States and the Centre. Such a council has yet to be formed though it is envisaged in the Constitution.

Appointments of Governors, etc.

Selection of an appointee depends on the requirements of the job, and the confidence that can be placed in the appointee by the superior authority. The Governor once appointed is not bound to abide by the views of the Central and the State governments. Governors have only to obey the requirements of the Constitution and their own views about the good of the State and the good of the country. Only in times of emergency or when the State ministry is not functioning and the President has taken over the administration of the State in question, he becomes fully answerable to the Central government. While the State Cabinet is functioning, the Governor has to be guided in all matters pertaining to the activities of the State government by the advice of the chief ministers. When the Centre and the State are ruled by the same political party, the functioning of a Governor does not become an issue between the two governments, only when different political parties are in the saddle at the Centre and the State, the problems arise because of the inadequacy of the conventions governing the functioning of the Governor. The Governor will not have a prior declared response to every eventuality. Perhaps there could be a permanent committee for nominations to high posts almost like the independent Election Commission (but with multiple membership) that will recommend, at short notice, through *ad hoc* nomination panels, a slate at least of three names for each high post referred to them. Such a panel while nominating few names for governorship should also have personal appointees of the Centre and the State in question as members so that the nominations are realistic. All appointments of pseudogovernment agencies like public sector chairmen or managing directors, vice-chancellors of universities, chairmen of arbitration bodies, etc., could be processed through expert panels set up by a hligh level appointments commission. This commission will be independant of the

Union Public Service Commission.

Any high-level job with more than one line of hierarchy is quite a difficult affair. No amount of bureaucratic rules and regulations can obviate future difficulties and problems. But the chosen person will have the necessary qualities of objectivity and firm pursuit of public interest along with the desirable qualities of earnestness, sincerity and wisdom. The working will become smooth as the conventions grow and political parties in India also learn to live together after the visible failure of single-party dictatorships in many countries.

One of the sore points is the provision of reservation of State legislation for the President's consideration by the Governor. Such reservation should be made only for specific purposes as envisaged and enumerated by the Sarkaria Commission. As a matter of salutory convention, such Bills ought to be disposed of by the President within two to four months of their receipt by the Union government. Any ordinance issued by the State government after a maximum of one re-promulgation must be replaced by suitable legislation. The Bills having a bearing on concurrent subjects or likely to come in conflict with Central legislation or go against constitutional provisions alone should be referred by the Governor to the Central government. The Governor could directly consult State or Central experts on these matters before formally referring such legislation to the Central authorities for concurrence/comments.

6

CONFLICT PREVENTION

Introduction

CONFLICTS WILL always arise, but as soon as an inkling is there or the conflict surfaces, every effort must be made to remove the irritants or to prevent the eruption of the conflict. Progress lies in conflict resolution, not in the absence of a conflict nor in its continuation. The situation throws up new leaders who apparently might be hot-headed and slogan-mongering rabble rousers. They could distort the reality and soon be joined by time-serving self-seeking gentry out to make easy gains and put peaceful people to ransom. Still the germ of the conflict must have already existed and contaminated the ideas of the opportunistic minds. Machinery should exist for speedy identification of complaints and discontent that usually can be removed by timely corrective action and sympathetic listening. Just like the resort to professional counsellors for domestic peace, appropriate groups and potential disorderly elements must receive appropriate counselling from the police and other public services. The law and order and planned development should be continuously kept before the attention of the student community which usually provides the unthinking force to the propagandists of disaffection. Mob violence is sometimes used to impose servitude on groups which are sought to be intimidated, as the Sikhs of Delhi after the murder of Mrs. Indira Gandhi.

The spark of conflict lies dormant in the people's minds and should be fought as if it was the forerunner of a raging fire. Even 30 years before the advent of Bhindranwale with his gospel of rule only by the Sikh militants, there were slogans painted on many Delhi street walls that the Sikhs were a separate nation, signed by some Sikh Brotherhood. It is the Delhi Sikhs who looked at these slogans with equanimity and later lamented the reaction against them after the murder of Mrs. Indira Gandhi. It would have been the right time 30 years ago to organize the Sikh minority at least outside the Punjab against such slogans. When Nepal and India were at about the same level of adversity, the open frontier for the Nepalese to come and go was quite in order. Now when there are more avenues of livelihood in India, the Nepalese who have made their home in India or who had been residents of the Indian part of the area, inhabited by the Gorkhas, want to be considered as full Indian citizens with their names on the voters' lists in India. Their outcry when they were not granted the voting right in certain Indian States assuming that they must be temporary visitors from Nepal should have been handled with understanding and sympathy long ago and not left to grow into the violent Gorkhaland stir contained now with considerable difficulty and violence.

Now Ladakh has been promised a backward area status, which is very statesmanlike on the part of the J&K State and the Central governments. This is the time for the Muslim minority of India particularly outside Kashmir to project the advantages of a secular State to their co-religionists in J&K or there may be more needless conflict. J&K state has the most advantageous status in the world, of freedom, security, in an autonomous region of secular India which also has practically the second largest Muslim population in the countries of the world. Wahabi puritanism must have suited certain countries at certain times when these were at the *nadir* of their fortunes ascribed to the diversion from the straight and narrow path of *Koranic* injunctions. True religion is in piety and social duty. Meditative philosophy of the *Sufis* with roots in Islam arose in Persia and Central Asia and found refuge in India where there was a kindred chord in the *Bhakti* movement.

Ramanand, Kabir, Dadu, Kamal, Nanak, Surdas and many great devotees of the world helped the composite Indian culture to grow. Islam really spread in our land on the shoulders of great *Sufi* saints. All this success was later usurped by the *Mullahs* and it served also the colonial masters to keep the people immersed in hair-splitting ruts than in God dedicated moral life. The Indian religions place much value on the pious life and the soul's aspiration to realize God. It is about time that the Muslims of India shake away all lethargy and pursue the *Sufi* path again shorn of any unwanted rituals not truly *Sufi*. Virtuous life can and should be propagated by the religions (without any ambition to proselytize) to mixed crowds. Ashoka's rock edicts are excellent examples of applied religion in an enlightened realm. Ashoka pointed out what is right conduct and gives examples how he conducts himself. It is not that Hindus (of all hues) worshipping all the different gods as chosen benevolent faces of the same true God and Muslims, with an excellent moral code and *Sufi* strain, cannot pray together publicly. It is very likely that their language of prayer is different and expectations too, but, in our growing unity, such elementary steps as the stringing together of a common prayer *routine* to the same God at least on their holy days should be taken. We must bring the two communities consciously together, otherwise Meerut-type conflicts cannot be prevented.

Communal conflicts cannot be resolved by an *Akal Takht* or a *Shankaracharya.* The solution lies in joint activities, discussions and dialogue, and respect for common national goals and ultimately mutual devotion as in a workable marriage. The majority vote will only suppress a conflict. For resolution a patient consensus has to be worked out. Democracy in reality means respect for the views and desires of each member. In any controversy, a scientific method may help take only an interim decision till a more acceptable one emerges. Opposition has to be won over or given due attention and should never be ignored. We have seen how an insignificant group in violent opposition can harm the nation as is happening in Sri Lanka by the activities of a handful of LTTE.

Conflict prevention is practical conflict resolution before it becomes violent. Victory in a conflict resolves the conflict by the rout of one side and revolutionary changes for both sides. The allies were victorious in the world war, but at great cost to their own countries. Our concern is to present conflicts as a temporary phase which can be sublimated to revolutionary synthesis for progress. The merging of viewpoints can occur only if the channels of communication are always kept open. The paramount interest of the nation or humanity must also exist among the opponents. The new specialist conflict managers would be trained as diplomatic messengers and trustworthy counsellors for sanity and peaceful progress. The third party is useful not as a judge or arbitrator but as a respected sage. He may even get the two sides agreed on a proper arbitrator.

An interesting case has been of India as the third party for conflict resolution between the Tamil Eelam protagonists and Sri Lanka. The ethnic Tamils and the Sinhalese had been complaining and then there was communal carnage in 1983 and a regular rebellion soon after. The third party was asked to help the warring groups disengage and proceed together to build an integral polity with assured democratic rights to the ethnic Tamils whether in majority in an autonomous part or as a minority in the rest of the country. Soon India found herself in the thick of the fighting since the LTTE refused to disarm according to the agreed schedule and only desired to take advantage of the withdrawal of Sinhalese armies from Tamil majority areas where the Indian Peace Keeping Force was to keep a watch over the transition from rebellion to peaceful co-operation. Whatever the merits of Indian involvement in the fighting, the lesson is obvious that a recalcitrant party which does not honour agreements may need deterrent action and the role of the third party cannot just be a picnic. The mediator must be backed by resolute will and public opinion. Mediation in open fighting or continuing tyranny should, if possible, involve also sanctimonious expressions from the weapon suppliers to both sides and the motivation for peace of the general public. Blessed are those that bring about peace and Americans must be given due credit for bringing South Africa and Cuba together and bringing the freedom of Namibia nearer, though they have to bear considerable responsibility for the intransigence of South Africa for the continuation of apartheid against the overwhelming world opinion.

The veto must not be used lightly for partisan gains of commerce and military outposts. Most countries should hand over such outposts to the local people or to the United Nations, as such outposts only create more tensions. Weapons trade should receive the searchlight of the international community just like the trade in narcotics. Iran-Iraq war and its prolonged mischief must be ascribed to the weapon supplying States. Any weapons disproportional to the legitimate need as, for example, recommended by future expert panels of the United Nations must be confiscated by the United Nations when it has assumed the necessary strength. This would be the first exercise in collective security for all. With great relief the arms race between the superpowers is hopefully receding. Such races anywhere endanger the security of the countries involved in it and endanger the world peace. Now is the time to mediate and resolve disputes sought to be settled by arms races, for example, between India and Pakistan or Libya and its opponents. Island nations in the Pacific Ocean should be assured cessation of nuclear test explosions in their neighbourhood.

Autistic Fears

Half the time the conflicts arise or are fuelled by autistic fears. When there is deep down a feeling of injustice inflicted on the other party or some such guilt, there arises fear of retribution or revenge from the other party even when that party is quite contented with *status quo* or desires to improve the existing relations. The speech by Churchill that set the United States on a confrontationist posture was partly of this nature, though the Soviet Union all along acted from its own feeling of encirclement. One is constantly surprised how India and Pakistan continue to share NAM and SAARC forums when they constitute a classic example of mutual autistic fears, one from the excesses of partition days or the size of India and the other from the record of Pakistani aggressions and drive for nuclear weapons. Even a baby can tell that they are treading the path of mutual harm. Common men and women on both sides of the border have so much mutual regard and feeling of kinship that the political enmity seems like a disease requiring immediate attention and a cure. So long as diplomacy will continue to place trust on lies and false declarations, there is little hope. Perhaps meaningful projects under the auspices of SAARC, exchange of visitors, expansion of commerce, etc., might place the nations back on the rails of mutual trust. I was surprised when a learned man from Pakistan expressed his country's complete ignorance of Indian religions and philosophy, he was so involved in the completeness of the Islamic faith for an average person in their country or perhaps anywhere in the world. This could make them even more withdrawn from contacts and communications and become more prone to autistic fears.

According to Pakistan, the main reason for their unhappiness with India is their claim on Kashmir. They believe that according to the Muslim League of India's pre-Independence days, Pakistan was formed as a homeland for Indian Muslims and the contiguous areas of Kashmir where the Muslims constitute the religious majority should become part of Pakistan and, by denying Kashmir this opportunity, Pakistan has been wronged. The actual historical facts are different. In spite of the slogans of the Muslim League the partition took place only because of the wishes of the British Indian provinces as expressed by the overwhelming majority of their legislatures and where the vote was divided, the province was also divided. The rules for the princely States were different which were to accede to the dominion of the rulers' choice if the adherence could be sustained from various considerations. The ruler of Kashmir chose to merge his State with India, and only a little earlier the effective political party in the State had repudiated the overtures of the Muslim League in no uncertain terms. Still the Indian Union gave almost a unique autonomous status to J&K and the populace repeatedly elected nationalist governments of the State and the ruler was deposed like the rulers of other Indian States in a constitutional manner. The decision correctly taken in those days cannot be reopened as that would mean outsiders dictating the internal affairs of this country. Islam being the reason for a separate nation is repeatedly disproven, e.g. even the original Pakistan could not hold together because of the rebellion of the major constituent in population, viz. Bangladesh, or look at the long-drawn-out war between Iran and Iraq, both Muslim majority countries. Let us refrain from rewriting the history of partition of India and seek fulfilment in co-operation instead. Kashmir could still be the Switzerland of South Asia drawing tourists and staying free from the fraternal conflicts of the sub-continent. Shortsighted populism of elected government in J & K has bred disillusionment and there is a terrorist movement nourished from Pakistan active there. The new mesures of responsible but good government will prevail soon, it is hoped.

Autistic fears are the opposite of superman complex and both breed antagonisms. *Anand Margis* were probably the first terrorist breed of supermen who felt themselves to be the only well-equipped persons to rule over others. Same can be said about the Sikh terrorists who wish to deny any rights to minorities or persons other than their kind of Sikhs. The great Sikh community has to bestir itself to show them their place due to their denial of basic values of the Sikhs or the traditional secular values and middle path of the Buddha and the *Gurus*. Discrimination against Sikhs in India was a myth started by the commercial interests amassing lucre out of refugee admission of Sikhs in the western democracies and providentially supported by the short-sighted agitationist campaigns of the Akali Party to snatch political power lost by them earlier through the ballot box. Sometimes we hear that the Sikhs have autistic fears of losing their identity in the vast population of India. Not only the things of beauty but also things and ideas of value last forever. The Parsis, the Tibetan Buddhists have not shown any sense of defeat in the diversity of India.

Temples of India and Some New Steps

India is a secular country where everyone is free to pursue and practise his faith or lack of it. The Hindus do not worship an idol which is broken or mutilated. New idol will have to be installed and special religious ceremonies are performed inviting God to particularly be responsive to worship of that idol in that temple. In a way God is invoked to regard that idol as one of His many ears and eyes for meeting the desires of the devotees. A Hindu temple if desecrated can again be sanctified by religious services and devices. Probably same holds for a Christian place of worship. Muslim, Arya Samajist or Sikh places of worship remain so under all circumstances and can easily be prepared for worship, since their sanctity lies in the assembly of worshippers than in any superficial symbols, though certain symbols are held sacred and do exist. The tombs and *Samadhis* of Muslim and Hindu *pirs* and *sains* are almost worshipped as the idols in a Hindu temple without any scriptural sanction but popularly regarded as the sure window of God on earth since, like Christian Saints, the *pirs* and *mahatmas* are believed to live forever for intercession in favour of mortals.

In India many religious places have changed the nature of worship depending on the change of the congregation. This is universal as most people would not like a house of God to decay or to be put to a mundane use. Such a background should be with all if they wish to resolve the Babri Masjid-Ram Janamabhumi temple controversy. Since everyone admits at least in India that the God of all religions is the same, there really should be no difficulty in anyone performing his worship in the same building provided this does not disturb someone else's mode of worship. In the recent past even two persons from the same family could not eat next to each other and required special earmarked individual place on the ground. Now even strange:s can eat in the same place and share the dining table. This also imposes some mutual etiquette. Worship in the same temple could become easier, if first certain secular temples are built and organized for such multiple forms of worship. The *Bharat Mata* temple at Haridwar is partially an example. Only the secular temples need not have any name of a principal deity attached to it, though in that sense *Bharat Mata* cannot be called a deity. It should not be difficult for the religion architects to design suitable buildings for common worship meeting the absolutely essential directions laid down in the religious texts for the distinct places of worship. Purely restricted rites may be performed for any religion at reserved times and occasions but keeping admission into the worshipping congregation open to all. We mean, if the congregation is to stand up or to bow in a standard fashion, all those who participate in the worship must also do so except perhaps a fully evolved person like Guru Nanak who did join congregations but would not do as the others because he was too sincere in his worship and noticed sham in the surroundings.

The most unobjectionable common worship like meditation before the *sanctum sanctorum* or the shrine as in Japanese Shinto shrines or offering of flowers as in Hindu temples or offering of charity as in Gurdwaras can be done by all at all times in the suggested secular temples of New India. We know that during any meditation including the silent reading of *Namaz* in the mosque, bells and music are regarded as distraction while in most other forms of temple, Gurdwara, or church form of worship, ringing of bells or music is necessary ingredient. For our common place of worship there will be no unwanted noise. The loudspeakers other than in lecture halls will not be used. In place of public address system, notices on silent wired television can be placed at points near about. Services especially for various religions will be properly timed during day or night and the officiating priests will be fully trained in the ritual and sacred lore. The visitors must also be reminded that they were visiting a place of worship and not merely a place of tourist attraction. The best way to bring Hindus and Muslims of India still closer is to allow them common places of worship where they could worship according to prescribed ritual in the same building or hall or courtyard and have more occasions to learn about each other as human beings moved by the same spirit. Common worship of sometimes ancient factional gods is quite common now in Hindu temples and many temples are open to all devotees. The concept has to be widened for all humanity especially when literally Hindu *Dharma* is simply humanism. Certain pilgrimage places should be organized on humanist basis with the local priests encouraged to join in this endeavour in their own selfish interest and in the national interest.

Any traditional obstruction separating Hindus and Muslims of India should be deliberately demolished by the communal leaders. The distinctive and separate places of worship need not remain aloof like before. In many places of worship official bars unfortunately still exist on the entry of people of different persuasion. The bloodiest communal conflicts have taken place abroad between the Catholics and the Protestants, but now they can freely join in the church services if they so desire in any church. In India where we take pride in equal respect to all religions, some Hindus even cannot worship in particular Hindu temples like others. Muslims are allowed to enter only a few Hindu temples because often there is a notice debarring non-Hindus. On enquiry we are told that non-Hindus are not normally respectful to temple idols and it is never known if their utterance in the temple will be acceptable to Hindu worshippers. We feel there has to be better solution to this problem than the current isolation of the two sets of worshippers. There is no official bar on non-Muslims to join the prayer in the mosque, but the total ignorance among Hindus of the style and content of *namaz* make them shy away from taking advantage of the privilege since the temples do not reciprocate and Muslims almost regard it as denial of Islam if they were to choose to copy Hindu worship in a Hindu temple.

The solution is to have new joint places of worship so that they become more familiar with each other's religion and realize more closely the basic unity in diverse religions. Arya Samaj and the Christian church in India are experimenting in reciting the bulk of their prayer in the mother tongue. The *Bhaktas*, the *Sufis* and the Sikhs recite their worship in songs. We hope the temple Sanskrit and the *maulvi's* Arabic will soon be replaced or supported by a lot of material in the mother tongue of the congregation. For the Punjabi language, the essence of Hinduism in spite of the pedantry of certain critics exists in the *Guru Granth Sahib*, the holy book of the Sikhs, and many Punjabi Hindus and Sikhs recite their daily prayers in Punjabi from the *Guru Granth Sahib*. Religious integration within the families had already taken place in the Punjab and that is how the Punjabis have withstood the onslaught of terrorists among the Sikhs. About 50 years ago or earlier in this country, in a typical Punjabi Hindu family, the *Gurbani* and *Ardas* were recited in the morning and the *Aarti* was sung every evening. On Thursday evenings, an earthen lamp was lit in honour of a local Muslim saint in a special alcove and on Tuesdays and Sundays, visits were made to the city temples or Gurdwara. Now-a-days such a composite routine for religious worship is quite uncommon. In order to encourage more intimate knowledge about different communities, it is important that places of common worship are set up as early as possible.

Common Ethics

Ritual is a well-recognized ingredient of religion. Ritual simulates sacrifice in detail. Ritual, however, must not be regarded as the core of a religion. It is only the packing of the ethics and philosophy of that religion. So-called fundamentalists are only the ritualists of any religion. They are not in touch with the modern reality and present needs of the human soul. They would rather cash on the ignorance of the flock and assume leadership by masquerading as genuine believers, because they have mastered the motions connected with the rituals. The core of a religion is faith and ethics of prescribed right action in social and human relationships. The religion guides each individual also in his purely personal quest of reality and fulfilment. Ethics is universal. Ethics has pragmatic as well as philosophic value. Ethical qualities enable one to command confidence of others in even worldly dealings.

No ethical person can have dual standards, of being honest and truthful only to his correligionists and being unjust and cruel to others. Feelings of brotherhood for the believers and hatred for those outside the pale only carry forward the ancient clannish and tribal origins of society. Even when certain practices are repugnant to another group, a *modus vivendi* is easily arrived at by everyone carrying out his duty in an unostentatious manner and without blatantly hurting the susceptibilities of the others. The barbaric human sacrifice gave place to the sacrifice of animals and this was sublimated to offering flowers and cereals. The exhortation to sacrifice for God (or humanity) is there and the form will continuously evolve and change with times and with ideas of the people concerned.

Kabir has extolled the virtue of charity. The concept of a Welfare State can be approached from the socialist angle as well as from religious insight. The *Sant-Mut* (faith of the godly – Hindu, Muslim, Christian or Sikh) is certainly a common heritage of all and one can see this in the common adulation enjoyed everywhere by the *sadhus, yogis, fakirs* and *ragis* of various faiths.

Truth has been interpreted as God by Gandhi and it is part of the national motto. No religion advises its followers to be restrictive in the pursuit of truth. If in spite of all this, we find so much deficient practice of truth, we must clearly grasp that, for many of us, religion is only a fig-leaf to cover our hypocrisy. The cult of group limits must give way to large horizons embracing the whole nation and then the whole of humanity. If one only were to listen to preachers of genuine religion from any label, one is bound to be impressed by the common ethics that is preached, only often the examples are given from one set of heroes and great men (of the religion of the preacher). This can be corrected when the training of preachers of each religion is carried in a secular way, that is, he is made familiar with the lives and examples of great and pious men of other religions too. In this context one can certainly offer tribute to All India Radio's Urdu Service which often gives authoritative talks on ethics with quotations and illustrations from all the great religions in the country. The talks are directed to Urdu-knowing listeners, perhaps a large number of them would be Muslim, but such talks are not available in other languages or directed to other religious groups.

Sectarian Pockets

Some *Gurus* or recently activated sectarian movements start colonies for their members and hope to practise better their religious rituals and self-help co-operative activities. So long as self-culture is the aim, and overweaning pride for their own state of bliss compared to other ordinary mortals is kept in check, such co-operative activity makes better citizens and human beings. On the other hand from a feeling of peculiarity in a crowd of strangers, some Hindu and Muslim enclaves grow up in differently labelled populated areas. This kind of self-invited ghetto mentality is against good sense as well as national aims. A good neighbour is a good neighbour whatsoever his religious label. In fact, having only correligionists as neighbours is injurious almost like inbreeding. The mixed locality should be the ambition along with mixed secular education. The existence of such ghettos is only the reflection of communal strife of the past few decades. Earlier, this was only an exception or pretty much based on convenience for the business or work of the residents. There could be conscious and deliberate bringing together of insiders and outsiders of such enclaves by celebration of fairs and festivals and advertised invitations for picnics and entertainments there. Sunday markets or sports events can be an attraction for the majority community to the suitable sites in the minority enclave. Religious *kathas* and *qawwali* programmes can also be a mutual attraction and occasion of common participation. Common people should stand together to oppose fundamentalist belittling of prayers at tombs of saints or public display of idols in processions, etc., outside the walls of the temples. A folk religion can lead to spiritual ecstasy much earlier than pretentious engagement in ritual and periodic prostrations in prayer. Organized religion in India should understand its chance of growth in the climate of freedom and secularism and invite others to join in discussions and other programmes since piety and charity is common to all faiths.

Instruction of Priests and Preachers

In India the gigantic task of educating our millions and billions has been too much for the government-run and government-supported schools and the government is inviting all kinds of groups often with considerable grants from the government. In fact some critics complain that running a school in a city or in excellent resort surroundings is now lucrative business since the parents and the government are willing to contribute to public schools. Since India is home of many religions the school syllabus and the text-books must not include material which is controversial. The children should be given education in ethics and even if there is a slant towards one religion, teachings of other religions should also be favourably highlighted. Ordinary schools even when run by distinct denominations should not be teaching priestcraft, for which there should be separate institutions. Such theological institutions should be supervised by a new national council for religious instruction having various *gurukuls*, *madrassas*, seminaries, etc., affiliated to it for financial assistance, and this council should see that apart from mastering the rituals, etc., of their own religion, the future priests and preachers become aware of the national scheme in religious instruction and the advancement of knowledge. The *pathshalas* and *madrassas* are too distant from the present-day reality of India which is the home of diverse ideas and philosophies. The new priests should be able to officiate in the religious sense at the happy or sad functions in any Indian home even of one of a different religion than in which the priest himself normally operates. For obtaining his credentials as a priest, *Pandit* or *Mullah*, one must master the respective theology and faith as well as have some minimum knowledge of other rituals. Within the Hindu faith some of the Arya Samajist and Sanatanist *Pandits* can serve households holding almost any special consideration for a particular god, monotheists, pantheists or agnostics. Special effort should be made to make them familiar with customs and rituals at the time of births, deaths or marriages for

Christians, Muslims and others, so that a single religious guide is available when the population is so intermingled and there may not be a large enough number of people to afford a particular denominational priest. If we want to spread respect for all religions, best is to inculcate this in a clear manner in the priests and preachers of each religion through well-designed theology education.

Uncontrolled religious instruction to theologians has resulted in priests blessing the nuclear bomb or various weapons to be used in wars. Religion will shed communal overtones only when it is preached for life in an inter-religious environment or for personal salvation and equation with one's conception of God. Institutions of religious learning which are recognized by the national controlling body alone would grant priestcraft qualification to their graduates and the tax exemption on charities will apply only to such institutions. All charities should be accountable to Parliament which follow the wishes of the donors within national goals and interest. The instruction would seek to broaden the outlook by teaching philosophy, history of science, comparative mythology, etc., besides the history, philosophy, rituals, etc., of the religion in which the student wishes to have his basic profession.

Religious Administration

Hindu temples are traditionally administered by owners. Often the priest is also the owner. Except to live up to the public image there is no control over the owner regarding funds and use of temple's property. Sometimes this has led to mismanagement and extortion from the folk and the pious people. In principle the donations are for the upkeep of the priest and the traditions of the temple and of the priests. Certain temples had considerable property and income. Such temples are a rich resource for the owner, and manger and for charities. Some enlightened managers lived frugally a life of devotion to their ministry. Where people became aware of misspending and diversion of temple funds, there was an outcry. Some States have even taken over management of temples and temple charities and properties.

In the Punjab, the Gurdwara Act was passed which handed over management to an elected body from among the Sikhs. Many religious sects and *Gurus* have well-managed temples and charities on commercial scale and style. Some of the sects get large cash disbursements from overseas from the faithful Indians or foreigners.

Usually the funds are for charity restricted by the local receiving bodies for charitable institutions run by them. Christian missions have commendable record to their credit for service to the poor and sick of all communities. Critics, however, of foreign funding wish all such funds to be accounted to the tax authorities. Similar demands and protests occur even in the USA and other rich countries where church funds are sought to be held confidential between the donor and the priest who acts as mere agent.

India being sometimes used for all kinds of social and medical experiments under different innocuous nomenclatures naturally cannot blindly trust the incoming funds professedly for good deeds. When the deeds may be with discrimination against certain sections or sow ill-will among people, corrective or preferably preventive action has to be taken. Considerable funds are coming openly to the fundamentalist factions in certain communities which is not at all in the national interest. To avoid charges of preferential treatment to certain charities *vis-a-vis* others, it would be right to have Parliament look into all charities, Indian-based or otherwise. An All-India Religious Endowment Board could be appointed by Parliament of some respectable individuals as members who have had experience of service of the poor. This board would be entitled to receive all information from the elected or appointed or proprietary managing bodies of all religious places and endowments and would give advice and management assistance.

The Board's recommendations will determine the year-to-year budgets of such bodies. What we are suggesting is social control over a very desirable activity of pious people with minimum increase in bureaucratic subservience to the State or Central government. The appointed temple management boards in certain States are already being accused of bureaucratic subservience to authorities against the truly philanthropic and pious traditions of the princes who used to regard themselves as the first servants of the Lord and were respected universally for this. There are the wellknown innuendos about British missionary involvement in the Karen revolt in Burma and similar help to the Mizo unrest in India. Even the Khalistani terrorists are banking on donated or misappropriated charity funds from the Gurdwaras in India or abroad. India being a secular country, given to equal consideration to all communities, will not object to the flow of charity from abroad on religious appeal, but it would be quite proper to have legislative supervision for ensuring its proper use. Each sectarian society is to be encouraged to be secular in disbursing charitable services. All sects will benefit if the services are non-sectarian. Even the volunteers and employees in the charitable service agencies should be selected on non-communal basis.

Secularism cannot afford to ignore or leave alone religious organizations in the country since in the past some such bodies have created problems between the various communities in India. Whatever the genesis of a religious management body, it cannot fly away at a tangent out of the orbit of national interest. The overall supervision will ensure that the management bodies do not undertake to interpret scriptures wrongly and against common morality and loyalty. The interpretation and re-interpretation is the job of the respected pious men of faith and learning meeting in conclave and arriving at a consensus that can stand the scrutiny of others. The Parliamentary supervision would also obviate conflicts and infighting for the control of endowment funds.

Disputation

In the matter of new ideas, philosophies and new styles of worship and prayer, the Indian approach has been pretty much scientific, i.e., accepting the sincerity of the disputant and allowing individuals to make up their own minds about the new proposition. It was because of this tradition that Shankaracharya had the phenomenal success in the days of yore of poor communications to practically force the Buddhist doctrines to either retreat all over India or get assimilated in popular Hinduism. It is the same tradition that permits almost Hyde Park like atmosphere for disputants in the great religious fairs of India. Guru Nanak could receive praise when he advocated that all ritual was meaningless and spread his ideas and preached in the focal places like Haridwar and Puri of Hinduism or the Buddha could preach in Varanasi, the centre of the Hindu Universe. The religious debates used to be held like wrestling matches under the eyes of a respected referee and the victory was proclaimed by public acclaim. Once political power became associated with members of recognized religious communities in colonial India, this freedom to discuss and improve one's concepts of reality and eternity came to a stop as everyone was nervous about losing some members from the fold of his communal label. Now that secular India will not accept political play of communal strength, the disputed and lively discussions will naturally restart. Some fresh allowance will have to be made for tolerating simultaneous acceptance of different doctrines. This might take some time since at present even games of cricket end in near riots. We have to develop further the culture of accepting diversity not only among different individuals and groups but also in the behaviour of the same man at different times so far as his personal philosophy is concerned. The psychologists have affirmed that the human brain can function at different levels at the same time. In fact, this kind of internal resolution of differences or co-existence in the same mind is a sign of human development.

God or history does not need religion of men, it is the man who needs religion as it might help him evolve into a better man and a better member of society. All religious man legitimately contend on this score as to the success they could show in the people's lives from examples of ordinary men actually known to the audience. Schisms have a way of occurring and then confronting society often violently. A secular society looks upon schisms as an opportunity to progress through their resolution or co-existence since no doctrine can stay static in form or content. Meanings also change with the change in values.

Proper Names

How do people choose their names. A baby was to be given a name in Delhi. The south Indian grandparents wished to choose the name in the traditional manner. A popular guide book in Hindi was purchased and they looked at the names. The grandfather commented that how could one find a good name in the north when the guide book itself has hardly any nice name like Sundaram, Krishnan, Parameswaram or Karthikeyan, etc. Ultimately they fell back on their own memory and gave a suitable classical sounding name to the little fellow. The babies are born free of any communal, cultural or linguistic label, but are burdened or loaded for whole life with the faith and culture of the forefathers. From Indian proper names it is easily seen if the person is a Hindu or a Muslim. They have a very distinctive way of giving names to their children. No special entry in the proforma is necessary and the name itself in general shows either the person's or the forefathers' religion. Christians in India are more secular in this respect. They can have a Hindu, Muslim or west European sounding name depending on the religion of the first convert or the benefactor of the first convert to Christianity among the forefathers. Sikhs do have the middle name Singh, and so have many clans and tribes among other Hindus. But Punjabis both Hindu and Sikh sometimes have a simple first name which may just be a fancy place name or the name of a common object like a tree or a month, etc. There is also the influence of the State language, usually a derivative of Sanskrit, that is how South Indian names sound over-Sanskritized and Punjabi names under-Sanskritized. The distinction of Muslim names from Hindu names in India is surprising since in Indonesia where most of the population is Muslims many of the names continue to be in the ancient Hindu tradition. In India the convert to Islam was always confronted by a large population of non-believers and so the break was deliberately overt by an invariable change of name. When a *Guru* converts an American Christian to his beliefs, in general in spite of there being no pressure to change the name, the new convert, for example, of Acharya Rajnish or to Krishna consciousness cult, himself asks for naming him afresh. Basically this is against the Hindu system of thought. Hindus do not particularly seek converts believing that everyone can evolve irrespective of which gods he may worship. It is very heartening to find sometimes in some modern family (Hindu or Muslim) now-a-days both Hindu and Muslim sounding names of brothers and sisters. We hope the fashion spreads and people start using proper names out of a whole infinity of names using Sanskrit, Prakrit, Persian, Urdu, Tamil or Punjabi, etc., and the present custom of announcing one's religion from just the first name withers away, and an Indian will have just an Indian name. This would assist the feeling of kinship of all Indian people.

We, however, are not in favour of any compulsion to choose only a particular style of names. In Armenia they tried to compel the Muslim minority to use only Christian style of names and created difficulties for the Armenian minority in neighbouring Azerbaijan. The use of family name (often the village or sub-caste name being used as the family name) began to be part of a proper name only few decades ago under the impact of European influence. Earlier, one had both first and middle names as given names in the north and for further identification father's name or the village name was used. In some parts of the South, the first name is father's name, middle name is the village name and the last name is the individual's given name. Since in future a person will be judged or valued for just himself, the father's name may lose significance and also the village name might become meaningless since more important might be the school where the fellow ripened into a grown-up citizen, or may be the political persuasion of each person becomes important and more rigid. Names of persons could be the names of most desirable quality or valued possession according to the parents of the child in the language of daily use. People might do away with the names of gods, goddesses, saints and prophets for their children which amounts almost to a blasphemy. The middle name often reduced the blasphemy, but already there is a trend to drop the middle name altogether. We feel that our proper names will evolve further, and no longer be loaded with religious identification.

7

SECULARISM

Introduction

THE DICTIONARY meaning of the word 'secularism' is having education independent of the control of church (organized religion). In India secularism has a wider meaning. Secularism here means separation of religion and politics, i.e. political parties must not attract people in the name of a particular religion or religious sect. A secularist belonging to any political party or religious persuasion shows equal respect to all religions. No religious act obnoxious to others is to be publicly performed where others can take offence. Almost every religion now in India has this secular kernel. Innumerable gods and goddesses in different climes and cultures basically manifest the same reality. The middle path and the right path as preached by the Jains, the Buddha and the Vendantists became the universal common thread in all Indian religions. The *Gita* summarized the approach by declaring that all religions lead to the same God, or same bliss. Muslim *Sufis* and Christian men of God have also the same view. In India there is accent on moral education good for all citizens even when controlled by a particular church. Sometimes, in misplaced zeal, education controlled by organized religion lays excessive stress on particular rituals and there can be an undercurrent of contempt for non-conformists and non-believers. It is on this account that in a multi-religious and secular society, all education even when in church-run schools must be overseen by duly elected governments of the States and the country. Religious ill-will and intemperance will not be tolerated.

Faith

Religion has grown out of fear, reason and hope. Fear of the unknown, fear of the future, fear of fate, accidents, illness and fear of many kinds, rational or irrational, was at the root of reasoning that built religion in order to kindle and nourish hope. A reasoned way to overcome fear is to build the feeling that an unknown benign power could protect one as probably was within the experience of the tribe or the community. This led to faith, religion and prayer and to the conception of all powerful gods and then the highest God. Faith could kindle hope and faith could give strength to bear adversity. Fear and hope led human beings, howsoever they might be isolated, to invent religion.

In India when the population was two hundred million, there used to be a folklore that 'there are two hundred million gods in the universe. The common man thus expressed the profound truth that each person had a distinct conception of god. The *modus vivendi* of our people and their gods had to be that faith and good life are important and it did not really matter which god one worships or which religion one subscribes to. Otherwise, fanatics of different beliefs would come to blows as happened among European gentiles and Jews, Catholics and Protestants, or Shaivites and Vaishnavites in certain South Indian areas in olden times. The saner view as preached in the *Gita* or held by the *Bhaktas, Sufis* and saints became the Indian philosophy of religion. Narrow sectarian beliefs only bring about widespread unhappiness. Faith and religion, however, prescribe social duties and social relationships. Once these become over-exclusive, one would be on the road to fanaticism exciting suspicion and strife from non-believers. Religious interaction and social duties usually are restricted to relatives and neighbours. Though this is not in the scriptures, yet often the social interaction is mostly with co-religionists since the priests know that the searchlight of modern thought, especially of others, will question the faith of their flock and the rituals as carried out by them. The restricted rituals do not suit present-day reality since our society is multi-religious and our social relations must extend beyond our co-religionists, especially the political relations which are the source of power for any leadership. The priests and such classes can make use of the free public relations opportunity to whip up support for themselves as custodians of their religious group which they can pretend to be in danger from non-conformists. The priestly class usually allied themselves with the exploiting groups and aspired either to be 'kings' or king-makers. It is such action which makes progressive people decry mixing religion with politics. Political power has to be used for national security and social and economic well-being of all the people inhabiting the country and cannot be assured piecemeal for separate religious labels. True men of religion are always the salt of the earth and great assets of a nation. They can also make valuable contribution to politics provided they encompass whole humanity in their vision and not just their own co-religionists. Mahatma Gandhi, Martin Luther King, Tutu, Agnivesh, Acharya Tulsi and Mother Teresa are examples of truly great religious souls. Faith is a great support for reaching any goal. Faith applied in negative ways can destroy. It can lead to sublime poetry, sacrifice and fulfilment, and it can also lead to inquisition and untold misery. Faith in *karma* and re-birth can lead to heroic efforts and sacrifice. It can also lead to abject surrender to *status quo*. This is what, happened in India. With riches of literature, culture and philosophy, we also had untouchables or practitioners of untouchability and the whole country became a pen of iniquity. We hope the Hindus have emerged from slavery with chastened minds and proper perspective on *karma* and re-birth, in spite of the odd Shankaracharya, who has learnt nothing.

Holier Than Thou

Faith, intuition, communion with the unknown and inspiration have often created persons of great insight, of poetic and prophetic gifts and people have flocked to them and their teaching. Lesser minds identify their own crowd of worshippers/disciples as 'good' and outsiders as 'evil'. In order to foster distinctiveness, special symbols and insignias are adopted like long hair, circumcision, particular tufts of hair, large ear-rings, sacred threads over the shoulder or around the waist, white or yellow paste marks on forehead, shoulders or body, special cut or colour of clothing, etc. A new mode of greetings, like a password, is often invented. Worship becomes stylized and another ritual is born.

The next step is to complicate a simple worship and train 'experts' in such lore who have monopoly of the stage with the god or *guru* to brainwash fellow travellers or rather mesmerize them into their own special quality. Ultimately such a denouement leads to destruction of other cultures, like Central Asian civilizations in the 8th and 9th centuries at the hands of Arabs and Persians, and then this ended in the mounds of skulls erected by Mongols all over the Persian and Arab world. The priests who could reel off textual authority for even insignificant details of their prostrations and rituals became indispensable for worship and they often assumed political power either directly or behind the scenes. In a multi-religious society, unless checked from the start, there can be multi-pronged strife among such claimants to political power. But all such claimants are obnoxious because they ignore the whole nation and seem to care only for kindred groups. How could the worshippers of 'one true God', revealed to them only, relish the presence of other equivalent clergies. Thus begins the 'holier than thou' syndrome that leads to religious strife. The genuine enlightenment lies in the secular and the co-existence approach. Secularism as practised or believed in the Hindu view of religion and now by the whole country decries the 'holier than thou' feeling by advocating equal respect for all religions. One is tempted to relate an interesting encounter with a Catholic priest of limited learning at the time of the Marian congress in Canada in 1947. The priest was surprised that a grown-up and educated person like the author was not in the true faith. When I mentioned that I was a Hindu and Hindus too have produced well-known religious people, e.g. Mahatma Gandhi, his immediate retort was that there is no merit in going to hell in the company of others whosoever they may be if they are non-believers even like Gandhi. I suppose things have materially changed now as the Pope himself has publicly shown tolerance for other religions.

Priestcraft

Priestcraft is even older than organized religion. Priests must be there to guide the laity in the intricacies of the rituals of their religion and mythology. Very few sects officially have no use of priests though some others officiate on a temporary basis. Sikhs and the members of the Society of Friends (*Quakers*) can do without priests and they have a much broader view of religion. People come to pray but slowly become serfs and slaves of priests. Ammon's priests could pull down Tutenkhamen – the first follower of one God. The Brahmins became a powerful hereditary priestly class in India and by skilful compilation of mythology and incessant preaching saddled the people with a whole world of gods and rituals. Their belief about the progress of soul after death is almost the same as of priests of Ammon and the ancient faith lives on, not only among the Hindus but also among the Tibetan Buddhists and many people that came in contact with the Hindu thought all over Asia. The Buddha rebelled against priestcraft and rituals but divided the whole world into aspirants and the laity. Whole-time pursuit of salvation became unwittingly the Buddha's great innovation which influenced many religions including Christianity and certain Mohammadan sects. Since the Buddha preached the middle path, we assume becoming a monk must have been only a temporary routine for young students or their teachers. For example, in Thailand the young students are advised to live the life of a monk. A Buddhist monk was a member of a very strict commune, the *Sangha*. He did not possess anything but a begging bowl and all his past or new possessions were handed over to the *Sangha*. The *Sangha* became quite powerful and dabbled in politics. They also inveigled rich heirs into the monkish habit in order to lay their hands on their riches. There is interesting literature of folk tales which, for almost a millennium, places great virtue with the monks and nuns but later starts ridiculing and presenting them as misfits and dull-witted.

Many believe that the machinations of the *Sangha* were the cause of the resurgence of Hinduism absorbing the popular middle-path principles of the Buddhists. Hindus also began to have *Sanghas* for whole- time pursuit of religion, but these were for only a select few individuals. Wholesale merger of the Buddhist values into Hinduism led many to dub the great 7th century Hindu revivalist philosopher Adi Shankaracharya as a Buddhist in disguise. Among the Hindus, Brahmin is still the priest for the rituals connected with birth, death, marriage, initiation, etc., while the *Sanyasis* and *Yogis*, like monks of the Buddhist and Christian orders, do not come in the limelight but are supposed to keep track of changing values and changing meanings. It is on this score that Hinduism has a self-correcting and persistent quality. Christian priests look after their flock in a more systematic manner, while the role of Brahmin priests among the city folk is now marginal. The Hindu style of worship and ritual is so widespread all over the world and particularly in India that even Sikhs who have no need of rituals or priests, have also succumbed and have many kinds of attendants on the holy book as if it were a live Guru. Sayyads among the Muslims, who claim their descent from the days of the Prophet, are accorded in India almost the same status as that of the Brahmins. Muslims also have *maulvis* who teach and propagate the *Koran* and look after the welfare of the people attending any particular mosque for group prayers. *Maulvis* soon become the guides of the local Muslims in religious matters and nurture ambitions of having political power based on their religious leadership. Muslims also have traditional courts, primarily presided over by *Qazis*, for administering personal laws to those who ask for it.

Everyone, Indians not excepted, belongs to a particular religion because he happens to have been born to parents professing that religion. One becomes liberal, religious, secular, indifferent or fanatic by one's personal experiences, or from the positive or negative environment around him. Perhaps, in place of the conventional initiation into one's religion at a tender age under the guidance of the parents, a custom would arise in the modern age of one's own declaration at the age when one marries regarding his current choice of sectarian label, if any. This would then help him have a stable worldly life.

A short-cut to a high self-image is to inculcate feelings of exclusiveness and closeness to the chosen deity. This sometimes leads to special importance to details of worship and to pride and prejudice. Now that one-man-one-vote prevails for conferring political power, the ready-made daily or weekly opportunity to lecture to the folk gives the priestly classes significant power. They often encourage all religious conflicts and problems. It is important that in secular India training of all priests is arranged so as to keep national goals in view along with making them good religious priests. The priests would be trained to habitually treat all religions with respect and learn about the middle path and how it is practically the same as recommended and practised in all religions. They should guide the people to use the vote as part of political activity and not religious activity. Separating religion and politics does not mean that religious people cannot be politicians or vice versa; it only means that politicians must not be partial to a particular religious label.

History of Communalism

There could have been communal disturbances about two thousand years ago between the Buddhist *Sangha* and Brahminical forces or between Shaivites and Vaishnavites before there was the synthesis as portrayed in the *Gita*. This is only a conjecture cooked up to soothe the conscience of quarrelling communities of today so that they are reassured that communal strife is natural in multi-religious societies. In actual fact India had such deep conviction about *Karma* and re-birth, such simple way of giving up one *guru* or taking up another or having scriptures that often identify all gods with one another, that the scope for religious strife was not there. Philosophical disputations were encouraged and it was a spectacle for the common people. Social levels were regarded as natural and even the untouchables had no recourse to violent rebellion. Though the same historians interpret changes in the religious label of Delhi rulers as a result of Hindu-Muslim strife of centuries, the actual fact is that Turkish and Persian invaders had the upper hand and the locals both Hindu and Muslim opposed them but not to much avail until the Europeans quietly grabbed the entire country.

All through Mughal and Marhatta chronicles we often see the Indian chiefs – Hindu or Muslim – fighting each other for self-aggrendisement, but never do we find the Hindus and Muslims, say, of Delhi or any other town or village fighting a communal battle. There was oppression of the common people – Hindu or Muslim – by their own or the neighbouring ruler – Hindu or Muslim. Indians never found religions to be a matter for mutual violence though it could provide fertile ground for philosophical and metaphysical discussions which were further downgraded on account of the *Bhakti* movement. In India even the Portugese missionaries with official motives of conversion of the heathens by force, if necessary, were bid welcome, though this led later to disillusionment. In the 18th century, when the Europeans got acquainted with India, there had been violent political conflicts in India between rulers often of different faiths and often allied with one another irrespective of religious labels. The Europeans read in such conflicts the role of communalism since they were very much familiar with religious wars practically of extermination having been rampant in Europe.

The present-day historians only echo the European theories and do not realistically evaluate the evidence. Indians rarely wrote history. They indulged in literature : epics, poems, dramas, short stories. The *Jataka* tales are rich in material about the Indian society. Our creative writers have written about lives and loves and fights of our heroes intermingling freely with gods and goddesses. When the *Tantra* philosophy and rituals were in the ascendant we find the Buddhists, Brahmins and ritualists contending among themselves as well as with demons and living corpses and we meet professionals of all kinds. We see all kinds of bravery and knavery, but never do we come across communal strife of any kind. Even the true recorders of events, the Arab or Chinese travellers, only comment with much regard on the equal respect the society gave to all religious. Even they have not recorded any communal riot. They have uniform admiration for the spirit of curiosity and welcome to even alien philosophies and permission to all ideas to mingle and contend. It was this characteristic that allowed Muslim divines and *Sufi* saints to get established at many places especially the cities of learning in Bihar, Bengal, Lahore, Delhi, Lucknow, Ajmer, etc., and that is how Islam got majority of converts through disputation about moral and religious values of equality and strict monotheism. One can also extrapolate from the fact that Islam got established in the Hindu and Buddhist countries like Malaysia, Indonesia much earlier than the establishment of the Mughal empire in India.

Even the court historians and diarists in Indian courts in the Persian tradition, who normally must sing praises of their patrons, have written volumes about the goings on in the courts and kingdoms. But nowhere there is a mention of communal riots. There is mention here and there of excesses by local officials and redress by the patron kings. We often come across gifts of estates and cash to religious places of all kinds by rulers of even different religious labels. There is mention of merit appointments from members of various communities to very high posts. Some misguided Muslim rulers did impose discriminatory taxes on non-Muslims, but the imposition was soon withdrawn and existed only in restricted areas. Jawaharlal Nehru has called the Mughal rule as practically Mughal-Rajput rule.

It is only the 'modern' historians trained in the European schools who imposed communal angle on the entire Indian history primarily to serve the imperial purpose of Great Britain to set Hindus and Muslims of India by the ears. For a full hundred years, before the advent of provincial autonomy in 1935, the history books propagated every historical incident as fight between Hindu and Muslims whether it was the conquest of the Delhi rulers by Turks, or the Turko-Afghans by the Mughals, or the rebellion of Sivaji against a Deccani kingdom. The joint front of Hindus and Muslims during the 1857 army revolt was interpreted as obnoxious everywhere leading eventually to the welcome of the Company forces by the loyal Hindus, the loyal Sikhs or the loyal Muslims. After the grant of provincial autonomy along with communal system of voting (separate electorates) we start observing or hearing about the chain of senseless atrocities and chauvinism of each community at the expense of the local minority. The communal virus was transplanted from Europe into India partly because of the imperial policy and partly because of the misinterpretation of India's multi-religious reality as that of continuous strife, rather than of mutual enrichment. The only way to rid ourselves of communalism is by a massive inculcation of secularism and practice of democratic consensus.

An authoritative creed obeying a single authority like the Vatican or a Mao leads to opposition, silent and suffering or vociferous and rebellious. It is the dictatorial organizations in Europe that brought about communal conflicts there. In general Indian religions or their pontiffs did not exercise such exclusive domain over people's minds. The ancient-most doctrines of suspended judgement and probabilistic nature of reality of the Jains were well established and affected every -one. Disputation and democratic acceptance of truth in an assembly was a well-known practice. Kashmir kings became converted to Islam purely because they came across very persuasive preachers of Islam. Co-existence of different faiths and philosophies in the same family could happen without attracting particular notice or scandal. Within the Hindu fold there is a spectrum of beliefs from atheism to pantheism. Kingship was hereditary whether the ruling family was Hindu, Buddhist or Muslim. The rulers did not interfere with the beliefs of the public so long as the mutual obligations were well understood. The great rulers – Ashoka, Akbar, Sivaji or Ranjit Singh – all encouraged piety and the middle path. The *Gurus* and the *Pirs* preached the greatness and nearness of one God and they had the most cordial relations among themselves as devotees of God and path-finders for the public. Live and let live was the motto in religion unlike the environment of Europe where Jews were considered the embodiment of guilt by the Christians and the Catholics held all Protestants as apostates. Within Catholics and Protestants, the schismatic cleavage was often very deep. Schismatic cleavage exists also in Islam and they regard each other especially in so-called Islamic countries as un-Islamic. Among the Hindus it is impossible to find anything un-Hindu. Even the schisms of other faiths have been mollified in India by the environment of tolerance in matters of creed. The communal riots in India do not spring from any points of doctrine but are triggered by the quest for political power still believed to emanate from the religious vote banks swayed, it is presumed, by the chauvinists of each religion.

Unity in Diversity

India is a world in miniature with many languages, dialects, all kinds of beliefs, various varieties of personal laws, completely different eco-systems as well as differences in food habits, clothing and dwellings. The diversity in India is so obvious. The unity of India is apparent to the discerning eye. The footsteps of many teachers across the length and breadth of the country still echo in the observed piety, tolerance, charity and hospitality. In Indian literature, India is always treated as a unity being a specially chosen place, where the most fortunate of mankind dwell. The cultural unity has been strengthened by the political aspirations of the people to have single strong national State. With the political separation of Pakistan, Bangladesh and continued separate states of Nepal, Bhutan and Sri Lanka, the geographical size of Jambu Dvipa (the ancient name for the sub-continent) was about 30 per cent larger than the present Indian State which still is practically the largest single unitary Indian State out of all such earlier States in history. Even now, the cultural unity of all these nations of Jambu Dvipa is evident in the villages. The string that unites is the prevailing traits of tolerance and humanism and practically a scientific approach to religion. These virtues can be summarized by the secularism that is practised by the peoples of India and other countries of the subcontinent, the imposed Islamization of a certain kind in Pakistan and Bangladesh to the contrary. Fanaticism will find it hard to take root anywhere here where countless humanists have lived and preached throughout the ages. Secularism is the key to unity in the diversity of the religious beliefs. Whenever India was great and strong in the past, its message was secularism. The Ashokan edicts speak only of piety and duty and not of any particular religion. The Buddha, Akbar or Gandhi talked of right conduct, and harmony with nature. Akbar even experimented with a nominal composite religion. Gandhi, Nehru, Azad, Vivekananda, Netaji and other makers of modern India were secularists to the core and visualized no place for communalism in free India. The Hindu word for religion is humanism. Jinnah himself believed in secularism for the free homeland for the Muslims. Faith is required only for fulfilment as a human being and all religion is only to help the human being to perform his duties that distinguish him from other creatures. It is humanism that suits human beings as their religious philosophy. Unity means harmony in diversity. Integration involves tolerance of cultural diversity and implies equality of opportunity. In certain multi-religious modern States of Europe provision exists now for the use of minority language and the use of public funds for the educational, charitable and religious purposes. The minorities are associated with the administration for these purposes. There would be local autonomy in scholastic and religious matters. Minority community managements will look after the funds for minority-run schools. This is also the present situation in all Indian States. Only in India, public funds are nowhere earmarked for religious purposes. However, in India special efforts are afoot to nourish and preserve tribal culture along with progress unlike Australia where aborigines were legally debarred from normal employment.

Strengthening Secularism

Indian philosophy is the foundation for our secularism. The belief in after-life, a guarantee of reaping what one has sown, finding virtue in charity and in hospitality are wide-spread. There is never any insistence on uniformity, but there is uniform respect for piety and the middle path. The scientific basis for God (in group consciousness and *satsang*) as well as direct mind-to-mind cognizance is hinted. For the common man prayer to any god, holy object, holy place, tomb or *samadhi* of a saint-hero is part of religion. Prayer is a unifying activity for all Indians. Every religion has a niche in Indian philosophy. Modern secular education has no need to involve itself in the rituals and intricacies of any specific religion or of sectarian worship in school. The students could be instructed in the rudiments of Indian philosophy and the foundation of religious life. The religious education in schools must mean understanding of the ethical values and the ability to gather information for making proper choices.

The belief in the after-life where one may reap the harvest of deeds of this life is a watchful policeman for ensuring conduct within limits set by society. This did foreclose all unrest and rebellion against social injustice in the olden days. There can be no scientific basis or proof of re-birth or other-worldly life after the day of judgement, nor can there be a scientific proof to the contrary. Scientific approach must be instilled into the child from the very start of its education. The Buddha, Swami Dayananda and the Dalai Lama have all insisted that one should accept only that teaching that gives conviction. Hazrat Mohammad asked Muslims to seek knowledge wherever available. The *Koran*, however, has sufficient knowledge for anyone to lead a good life. Christ and the Sikh *Gurus* were against a mere religious facade, but desired a religious person to be spontaneously pious and humanist. Lessons in secularism could be planned in the study of literature, history and philosophy. The children must be exposed to an environment of tolerance and easy access to different kinds of worship and taught about the great men of many religious beliefs, who have served mankind truly. Temples, open to people of any calling, and debates of all kinds as well as discourses on religious topics for all will sharpen the secular minds. The scientific method and experimental approach to truth will give tremendous support not only to secularist ideas but also to modernization.

Modern Trends in Hinduism

Hinduism is an ever evolving religion. The Hindu word for religion is *Dharma* or natural quality and duty of a human being and the natural qualities are influenced by environment. Inter-personal relations change with times. Hinduism is not limited by the view of a single founder, a single holy man or a single holy book. Most Hindu thought claims a token kinship with the ancient *Vedas*. But in ancient times Jain and Buddhist philosophies flourished without accepting the authority of the *Vedas*. The Buddha himself had no place for the soul or God in his scheme of reality. The Buddha, however, preached the same practical religion which almost exists intact in Hinduism. With him human *sanskara* or individual impressions, on the void, of various lives of a being vanish when one attains *Moksha* or Buddhahood. Hindus say the same thing in different words that on the attainment of *Mukti*, the human soul merges in God giving up its identity and is liberated from the cycle of re-birth. There is almost common belief in the virtue of non-violence and vegetarianism, though Jains lay much more emphasis on these virtues. The Buddha was recognized as an incarnation of Vishnu long ago. Inter-dining and inter-marriages with Buddhists and Jains are now becoming possible for all through public eating places and court marriages. A Hindu finds it equally meritorious to worship in Buddhist and Jain temples. It is surmized that the Hindu view of Vishnu having incarnations for the benefit of human beings is a development of the *Mahayana* concept of benevolent deity helping and guiding people.

The traditional methods of worship with pilgrimages, circumambulation, prostration, flower offerings, lighting of candles, ringing of bells, etc., are almost universal, and unite all religions in a common mould. In Hinduism devotion and faith in some saint/*Guru* is considered of worth but the choice is left entirely to the intellectual and devotional evolution of the individual. This has kept the doors open to all including animists, tribals, snake worshippers, agnostics, even atheists, etc. The great majority believe in one supreme god manifest in many forms or unmanifest in any form. They define God as truth, consciousness and bliss to which even the atheists might agree as the definition of ultimate reality. Hinduism provides for the evolution of social and religious groups within its fold. For example only a few decades ago the worship of *Siva* and *Sakti* was accompanied by animal sacrifice and ecstatic orgies, but many devotees now have taken to offering only flowers and coconuts as in major worship of other deities.

In the 18th century there was considerable decadence and superstition rampant because there had been practically a century of anarchy and the learned had fled to distant safe places. Ignorance and superstition along with exploitation and untouchability were rampant. The restoration of Hinduism and its refurbishing were due to great reformers during the early stable colonial regime. Some of the reformers were Raja Ram Mohan Roy, Dayananda Saraswati, Dev Guru, Radha Swamy, Shivananda, Ramakrishna, Vivekananda and last but not least Mahatma Gandhi and Tagore. Teaching of the *Gita* has been emphasized by all and the perennial *Ramayana* and *Mahabharata* continue to be the favourites of the people. Dr. Radhakrishnan would, by far, be the best exponent of Hinduism in recent times. Hinduism preaches rational acquisition and enjoyment of one's possessions along with care of the needy and respect for all life. Asceticism was relegated to later life and is reflected in the exhortation for simplicity and against irrational consumerism. Among the Sikhs, the best exponents of resurgent Hinduism, systematic work in a worldly calling is a form of asceticism dear to the *Guru*.

Swami Dayananda proclaimed that anyone could be converted to Hinduism when earlier such conversions were not permitted. Many Hindu godmen who preach among Christians, etc., themselves do not seek converts and are contented that the disciples follow the religion of their forefathers more intelligently and they derive solace and fulfilment from it. Swami Ramakrishna, the one genuine exponent of secularism, practised in his own life various religions and proved to all that one could realize God through any of these ways.

After Independence, the reform movement gained momentum and its results got legal enactments. Untouchability and abetment of *Sati* are now crimes. Gullible people here and there are still made fools by certain fake godmen, but on the whole the Hindu belief in having a *Guru* to guide him in spiritual and ethical values is still strong. There are many holy men and women with their own disciples and who seriously attempt to remove personal doubts and problems of the laity. The Hindu Code Bill has conferred various rights on women and brought personal law in line with modern needs. Free and active press, cinema and modern means of communication have broken the back of charlatanism and superstition in the name of religion. The anti-secular factional fights are only the growing pains of the nation. Political power is still sought by local majorities in the name of religion since religious preaching gives a built-in edge for public relations to the priests and the like.

Hindu daily worship for the laity takes only a moment and is a renewal of prayer or promise. Listening to scriptures and religious discourses and participation in devotional music is considered meritorious. Most temples provide for all this. The great gatherings provide a Hyde-Park like outlet for religious observance or resolution of doubts or propagation of special views. In the absence of regular preachers to whom the flock must submit regularly, the Hindu places of worship are singularly free of political or fundamentalist exploitation.

The *Bhakti* movement is still strong and *Bhaktas* are often blessed with miracles before their eyes which are often not easily explainable unless one accepts certain happenings beyond known physical laws. With advances in science, even physics is becoming too big for being circumscribed by its own laws. Many godmen are expanding their following and the disciples start new chapters for group worship, usually once a week. There are all kinds of temples spread all over the country and Hindus find it easy to worship also in non-Hindu temples like Gurdwaras or the Buddhist, Jain or Christian places of worship. Hindus do worship Muslim *Pirs* and frequent their tombs, but the prayer in the mosque is so much a group prayer and involves actual silent recitation of prayers in Arabic that they feel strangers to it especially because there is no altar for individual prayer. Most Hindu temples contain idols and it is claimed that when a Hindu worships an idol, he actually worships one true God, one of whose god-forms is particularly dear to the devotee and his idol has been particularly consecrated that it becomes the ears and eyes of God such that the prayer can assuredly be heard. The idols are thus myriads of listening posts of the one God who is in fact everywhere and can be approached in the silence of one's heart.

The local temple is also the venue for social and cultural life of the neighbourhood. Many States have set up official bodies to streamline the management of the charities and the temples. Many modern temples have a multitude of idols to suit the individual inclination of the devotee. It is possible that soon in India there will be inter-religious places of worship and Hindus would naturally welcome this development.

8

SCIENCE AND RELIGION

Introduction

SCIENCE HAS a continuous quest for truth. New theories replace old theories when fresh observations or more convincing arguments favour the new ones. Every scientist is conscious that any solution is only temporary and must give way to a better one when it is forthcoming. Some of the passions in the world must cease if the scientific method is more widely applied and accepted. The method is based on unfettered and unalloyed observations and rigorous logic built on intuition and axioms in order to explain the known and to predict results of further experiments and observations. Only objective measurements are valid which can be reproduced by any other scientist with proper instruments and equipment. Any exceptional observation not explained by the theory is not ignored or kept hidden but is welcome for study of all factors that might explain the new data keeping the theory intact. However, if necessary, the scientists will jettison the old theory welcoming a better one with pleasure.

Dogmatic faith can have no scientific basis, though people have gone to absurd lengths to prove scientifically, i.e. by logic from certain axioms and observed complexity of the universe, the existence or the qualities of God, of life after death, of soul, reincarnation, etc. God in fact summarizes our ignorance of the reality, if any, behind the universe with the life that exists in it. The ignorance cannot become scientific knowledge just because a word has been coined for it. '*Ke sera sera*' (what will happen, happens) describes reasonably the universe without involving God, soul or logic. But reasonable consistency of any doctrine is not enough. To become religious belief, it must lead to individual and social betterment.

Progress enjoins changes in values and goals and new perspectives in inter-personal relations as well as in self-improvement. Science works for human welfare from understanding and new applications of materials and energy. Science for the present is only at the threshold of understanding the mechanics of the brain and how mind works in its control over the body, but the nature of thought and how one happens to think are yet beyond scientific reach. There is considerable pseudo-scientific literature about God and religion using the vocabulary of science, like the atom, vacuum, dual nature of particles and waves, black-hole, big bang, probabilistic nature of states, matter-energy equivalence, relativity, gravity, etc., and the vocabulary of religion like the *atma*, levels of consciousness, quiet of nothingness, the hum of the brain, immanence, reality, self, etc., and the verbosity is supposed to somehow translate religion into science. Science as well as religion only offer models in their own domains and, as models often do, these also have parallels. One can only say that the scientists and religious people can perhaps sympathize with mutual profundities since these are often analogous.

Scientific Analogies

There are macro- and micro-theories in science. For certain coarse phenomena, the atoms and molecules are just incompressible balls but at micro-level they have a complex internal structure containing ions and electrons, alpha particles and neutrons and protons. If we carry out experiments with particles at very high energies, we find that even the elementary protons and neutrons have structures. The smallest entity envisaged is a quark or a gluon and perhaps a graviton. These have not yet been encountered in the laboratory but are inferred to exist and form the elementary particles that constitute matter. What is a quark or a gluon or a graviton made of? Perhaps of a field of force or of nothing material. So all this universe is made of nothing (perhaps of God). From another direction all stars and inter-stellar matter eventually vanish into black-holes. What are black-holes, in one word – nothing, but some kind of field of force and these are not witnessed through any material or radiation properties. How did the universe begin? The scientific answer sounds like a religious chant. There was nothing and then there was a big bang and the universe began as an ever expanding and evolving swarm of stars and such objects, flying away from each other, to end in one or more black-holes. Black-holes might thus be agents of Siva, the God of destruction, and when somehow the black-holes get together to from a huge black-hole or a *Brahmand* of Hindu mythology, it explodes and creation starts. In a way from the apparent analogies the creation and destruction of the universe were intuitively explained correctly by religious seers much before science laboriously reached the same conclusions. Only the mythological conclusion is fixed while the scientific theory is open to change depending on new scientific insight. Like various levels of scientific theories, religion also exists at various levels to suit minds at different levels of understanding and preparation. The illiterate woodsman has only his family and tribe as his world and religion for him means obedience and trust in elders and participation in prescribed feasts and dances. The average house-holder having experienced buffets of fortune is keen to propitiate fate in obedience to traditional religious practices. He has learnt that virtue lies in good deeds, i.e. daily worship of the deity, reading or listening to pious literature and being a good child or parent or companion, etc. The meditating type indulges in silent communication with self or contemplates on the sayings of his *guru* or on the qualities stated to belong to God. He believes that the time spent on repeating the name of his god is time virtuously spent. According to Bernard Shaw, life must evolve to pure thought and contemplation. He has also given the analogy of square-root of minus x for God. Since x is unknown, any function of x is unknown and so is God. If zero is the beginning, minus figures occur earlier than the beginning, so has God existed before time began. The square-root of a negative number is imaginary and not real, same can be said about God. Lastly, the square-root of minus x when operating on itself produces a real number, i.e. minus x and so does God when He produces the real universe all by Himself.

Scientists have endowed vacuum with all kinds of qualities. Perhaps they have used the analogy of the conception of God from religion to define the qualities of their vacuum. Black-holes and space are manifestations of the vacuum. Scientists also claim that there is matter as well as anti-matter and these annihilated each other, but there is preponderance of matter. Here is a distinct echo of the concepts of God and Devil. An exalted religious person can delve into the depths of his mind and be inspired to uttering sublime truths and construct a special universe of religious lore, or mythology.

Science permits communication with the help of instruments to distant places and even distant planets and stars. Spiritually evolved people claim to have Extra-Sensory Perception (ESP) and communicate with similarly endowed people or can observe unaided distant regions by sheer accidental ability or through an acquired *Siddhi* through *Yoga* and meditation. Certain electrical engineers have studied ESP under controlled conditions and verified some of the claims.

Science regards reality to be a super-position of states and an actualization takes place when an observer interacts, just as a Hindu can simultaneously picture godhead in different ways and be all adoration when he enters a specific temple or contemplation. According to Pauling and Kothari reality must have both complementary principles of science and *ahimsa* (truth and non-violence). They adopt the panpsychist position that everything in the universe is conscious.

Aims of Science and Religion

The aims of science and religion are different. Science aspires to understand transformations in nature. A religious man hopes to get answers by purely thinking on the existence around him. This approach is not against logic. He has no means to experiment with the universe and can depend only on intuition, inspiration or revelation. A scientist must swear by verifiable observations and results, but the religious answers are to be taken as dogma on faith, and by definition are true. Religion attempts to give values and if the change in environment and change in lifestyle require new values there would be turmoil in people's lives until new revelations underscore more appropriate values, modifying the religious teaching where necessary. For a stable society, the cherished value, must assist in coping with life. Veracity, and persistence, are, however, some commonly recognized values. For scientific goals, personal morality of the science worker is irrelevant except that he must abide by scientific values of objectivity and logic as already developed by others or by him. A scientist works with the ambition of making a definite in-road on the prevailing ignorance, but he is fully aware that his contribution may be overridden sooner or later. Usually, the scientific theories are materially modified in about ten years or so.

This realization does not diminish his ardour or the importance of his contribution in the linking up of future advances. Religion is meant to influence the personal life of a religious person a great deal. His mind will be peaceful and full of hope for the future whatever, only if, according to his understanding of his religion, he has spent a good religious life and has been loyal to the values impressed on him by his religion even where such values were at variance with the particular values enshrined by other religions. Religion, however, involves also social duties, social acceptance and social involvement in one's personal affairs. If a person's religious beliefs and life are such as invite social rejection, the physical end would be woeful even if he were to sup in heaven after death. Great religious innovators and reformers are, however, not deterred by social rejection in their day. We have the lives of Christ, Socrates and Meera Bai as some examples. Such people live in the minds of their admirers and worshippers after they are gone. The religious works are for both personal satisfaction and regulated social intercourse. Godliness means love and total devotion. God gives faith, mystery and a personal infinity. Religion and God aim at offering bliss and perfection. Hell is there to restrain tyrants. Ethical principles are the human knowledge unknown even to Adam at the start. Science only works for a fistful reality at a time which is guaranteed to be short-lived, though it adds to the sum total of human wisdom.

Science and religion are not mutually exclusive. In fact many persons excel in both. Some religious aspirants have contributed to science, especially astronomy, seismology and medicine and many scientists have authoritatively propounded religion. Intense wish and persistent effort to succeed is common to scientists and the religious. There is hardly any difference between modern scientific approach to religion and that of the Buddha or of the humanism of the Hindu view of life. According to Einstein, science without religion is lame and religion without science is blind. George Bernard Shaw thought that poverty is the root cause of suffering, greed, monopoly, wars, priest-craft or kingcraft and ignorance. According to Goethe, the present-day nullity was on account of specialists without spirit and sensualists without heart imagining themselves to be at the summit of civilization. In fact the Charuvakian hedonism was rejected from Vedic times. The religious force and the ethical ideas of duties based on it has been a very important formative influence on human conduct.

There is still considerable divergence in the dogmatic religious perceptions and the scientific method. In the dogma-ridden religious pursuit, one is only hoping to follow others in the achievement of beatitude, he is not a creative aspirant who experiences happiness through intuition and a creative understanding of hitherto hidden mystery. We disregard fundamentalists as religious devotees. They are only immersed in rituals which are deluding them primarily for self-importance and perhaps political power. Ritualism under the tutelage of priests has been in existence from time immemorial or from pre-religion. Democratic exercise of individual's rights has impelled the busy-bodies of religions to expect political support of the faithful so that they can continue to exercise the traditional power which was at first regarded as accruing to them directly from God. Whenever a feudal society is attempting to become democratic and modern fundamentalism raises its ugly head as has happened in some Islamic nations, e.g. Egypt, Iran and Pakistan.

Science of God

Some scientists have given their ideas of God or the Reality behind existence. This does not mean that God has been reached by a group of scientists through their pursuit of science. This concept of God is only an extension of the scientific view of mind as an activity of living brain. In general, the view is that God as a Creator or controller does not exist and such a God is the creation of man's imagination in his own image. Man endows his God with perfection and other attributes. The scientists also affirm that since they cannot experiment in spiritual matters and most affirmations about these are a matter of personal belief or inner unique experience usually not reproducible by anyone else, science cannot really throw much light on the existence or non-existence of soul or God. Since there is substantive reality around us, one could always call the principles of physics and chemistry, psychology and logic, statistics and astronomy as the handiwork of God, to start and operate creation. Since man hankers after joy, society flourishes in truth or consciousness is the main non-material concept, and since civilization suddenly reaches the cross-roads of destruction through violence and is preserved through love and *ahimsa*, God is regarded as the sum total of such objectivized qualities and basics. Scientists are content with dealing with the concepts of particles and quanta and do not speculate with the religious divines in their affirmations or denials. Even when scientists speak about the atom and the *atma* they do not commit science to their statements. Most scientists have, however, agreed that the sciences do provide analogies which are parallel to the visions of the seers about reality.

Certain scientists speculate that replicators of genes have evolved survival machines, most advanced being the human beings. The machines' importance to the replicators is its longevity, fecundity and copying fidelity. Similarly the evolution of the capacity to simulate culminated in subjective consciousness. Religion, however, claims that the consciousness has an objective reality as soul and the integration of all consciousness is God. The individual human mind is an abstract pattern of memory, skill and experience. The consciousness of the mind is regarded as the information standing wave, 'a certain dynamic invariant in the stream of incessant transformation'.

One may advance a view about God from the growing understanding about the working of the brain. Brain is a material construct. Mind of man is regarded as different from brain, but is entirely related to it since it has no independent existence. Even when certain persons just resuscitated from almost death aver about the independent possible momentary existence of their minds, they are communicating only when the brain is back in action. Scientists are now examining how the thought processes occur and have a hunch that the co-operative functioning of many brain molecules constitutes the mind or, simply stated, the functioning brain means mind ready for action. It is the co-operative functioning with the activity propagating quanta moving along the nerves that constitute thought and consciousness. Extending such logic, we might speculate that the co-operative action of all minds constitutes God. The seers also believed that God and soul are not different in essence and the soul attempts to merge in God. Our view would be each mind (soul) contributes to the God Reality and the salvation of the individual rests in this realization thus understanding his firm linkage with all mankind. Such a scientific (pseudo-scientific) view of God will lead to most of the spiritual knowledge as a corollary. Even prayer can begin to have an objective foundation, besides being a psychological and self-development aid. For the common man faced with impossible desires and situations and often witness to sudden upheavals in the life of others, God is a Super Power who can be firmly influenced to help the individual in his own inscrutable way.

Metaphysics

Metaphysics deals with the philosophical questions about the super-natural while physics deals with observations and experiments pertaining to natural phenomena. The natural phenomena include particle reactions which can never be directly observed and which do not result in observations that can be explained on just simple causal logic. The theories down at the base are highly esoteric and statistical in outcome. The *qi* function of quantum physics and the quarks are only to be inferred from the statistical materialization of the square of the *qi* function or from the multiple agglomeration of quarks and gluons. The gravitational attraction is ascribed to gravitons which have not yet been encountered in physical equipment in the laboratory. The vacuum of space is supposed to be filled by a sea of particles which do not manifest themselves since they stay in 'negative' energy states.

We can say that physics is approaching the super-natural and is giving up mechanistic or 'natural' models. Metaphysics, on the other hand is trying to probe super-natural phenomena with the only instrument so far available, that is, through selected or trained minds. As the science of mind develops, metaphysics may get closer to physics. Metaphysics as a discipline of science (reproducible results and observations and necessary and sufficient theories leading to acceptable results and tests) had been established by the Indian *Yogis*. An individual can progressively be developed for metaphysical insight and he also achieves paraphysical abilities, and the well-known training steps lead to well-known control points in the form of insights and supernatural abilities, temptations, *Siddhis* and ultimately to intuitive identification with the Cosmos. Modern metaphysicists are approaching the problems connected with the super-natural through the familiar sciences of psychology, physics, chemistry, biology, etc. Hypnosis, selection of peculiar minds, and mental manipulation by *Yoga* like systems are, however, the only tools available to them. Science of the mind and artificial intelligence has to go far to create useful instruments for their work.

It has been established and anyone can convince himself that there is the phenomena of thought transference, telesight (extra-sensory perception), clairvoyance, etc., which cannot be given a natural explanation in terms of physical principles. Work is in progress at the Biological Science Department of the University of Pittsburg though there has been opposition to call such work as scientific. Work on psycho-kinetics has been carried on at the Mind Science Foundation at San Antonio in the USA and the Maimonides Hospital at the University of Virginia. Work on ESP is being published in communication journals by the Duke University and the Stanford University. A well- known paper is on 'A Perceptible Channel for

Information Transfer' by Path-off et al. in the *Proc. IEEE* Vol. 64, pp. 329-54. The only transmitter or receiver that is possible is the human mind. The radiation that carries information in ESP or in thought transference is known to be neither material nor electro-magnetic. Perhaps it is the *qi* function associated with matter as well as quanta without being material or energy. *Qi* being non-material exists for all particles or events involving energy, for all time and everywhere in the past, present or future. This non-zero function may be sufficient to excite resonance in a tuned or trained mind anywhere any time, thus causing awareness by 'super-natural means'. Thus, physical concepts might assist in understanding super-natural faculties of a brain.

Most religions ascribe consciousness to souls. Souls, however, are manifest only where a living brain functions. Recent psychological data collected from people who had almost died before regaining their ability to communicate indicate that the dying have an awareness as if they were observing their own bodies from a growing distance or as if the soul is distinct from the body. This could very well be the property of the dying brain that it interprets weakening of the senses as if there is growing distance between them and the brain. The visible light, etc., may just be the physico-chemical steps in the progressive extinguishing of the brain's activity. Religious thought is philosophic with roots in reason with the background of deterministic mechanistic models. The social goals demanded an idealistic view of life of want and privation. The soul was deemed everlasting and so this led to the theories of the after-life and ultimately to transmigration of souls.

If we can assign the statements of the Buddha and the Hindu scriptures on transmigration purely to logical beliefs and a flair for instruction, we would be left only with the microscopic recalls of previous birth or births. Perhaps this would be just freak duplication of a previous brain capable of amplyfying the *qi* function from the previous dying brain. There is no reason to expect that every brain will have a resonant brain in the future or every soul will have re-birth. In any case the souls cannot be countable since their origin and end is the infinite God. The earth certainly had no living being at one time and even the sage Bhrigu has not cast the horoscopes of all mortals. Logically we may have to build-in an ability to fracture Itself with God for the creation of souls. Will this be a quality or a failure? God only interacts with the qualities of brains since God is circumscribed by the human brain.

Metaphysics can progress only when artificial intelligence can duplicate the capabilities of sensitive minds. The drumming of a pot, miraculously writing pens and sticks that lengthen in the beard of the thief are all fake. Miracles are factual for the faithful. On an aside many performers of miracle admit these to be frauds for the bolstering of the faith. The miracle seeming juggler's feats may need verdicting by self-confessed magicians. Our concern here is with genuine super-natural phenomenon and not fake ones, but it is not easy to separate the grain from the chaff. There are genuine feats not easily explainable. A *Yogi* could instantly transmit the confidence and ability to walk on red hot coals to many ordinary individuals who happen to be standing and watching him treading on fire. This kind of metaphysical transference of super-natural ability is beyond logic or customary channels of transference of skills. There have been authentic demonstrations of metaphysical vibrations induced in inanimate objects without any visible means by a singing mystic. Metaphysics is concerned with performance of the human brain which is the most complex instrument in existence. Its known capability is more than that of a billion dollar computer. For further work in metaphysics a background of many sciences is required, e.g. of logic, philosophy, computer science, cybernetics, etc. Many developed countries are studying *Yoga*, telepathy, clairvoyance, telekinetics, life after death, etc. Violence and injustice may also be involuntary aberrations of the brain. A deeper understanding of metaphysics and the working of the human brain might improve the environment in the world to a utopian level.

Co-existence

Uniformity has been the ambition of dictatorships, glorification of non-possession and poverty the philosophy of scarcity; and sacrifice, the philosophy of hemmed-in revolutionaries. Now the ideas of uniformity in wretchedness must be given up with the promise of plenty from science and technology and careful planning along with the winds of new economic order and budding co-operation among nations. The fascists of Mussolini wanted to Italianize the Italian minorities for glorious uniformity. Similar was the fascist slogan of Indianization of Muslims. For uniformity, intellect's play has to be prohibited. During their aggressive expansion in Central Asia the newly converted Persians did not tolerate even most peaceful earlier cultures there and destroyed them out, root and branch. They did reap the whirlwind as within a couple of centuries mounds of skulls were built in their lands by the marauding Mongols. The intolerance further vitiated the relations between the major schisms of Islam which is still continuing. By suppressing variation, one does not preserve a tradition but according to the rules of evolution one destroys the whole. Further development in evolution has to be in the realm of ideas. Man is not going to grow into a more complex creature, physically, but he may develop new mental abilities. The dogmatists are so wrapped up in the past successes of their dogma that they will not brook further evolution in these. Mind, however, cannot be chained. It functions at various levels and can at the same time subscribe to different philosophies. Many ideas co-exist in it. Many isms and ideas must also co-exist in society so that different permutations and combinations are tried which is the base of creativity. The age of democracy encourages individual discriminating probes. If we wish to spread freedom, we cannot limit ideas to central committee dictates. Even Communist edifices are crumbling before our eyes. The Pope, a symbol of orthodoxy, is surprising the followers with the breadth of his outlook and adherence to the principles of co-existence.

In a country of diverse religions and philosophies like India, acceptance of co-existence of different religious views is naturally going to occur as an evolutionary step at this juncture. There will be natural mellowing down of exclusive practices. Personal faith of the individual can be left entirely to himself so long as it does not trespass on the peace and self-esteem of others. A summation would be preferable to obligatory synthesis.

Modern Man's Religion

Modernization of the environment alters the value system too and the modern man has to come to terms with modernization. He has access to much more information. People have freedom of speech and expression. There are no censors looking over his shoulder. Plays are presented on stage mixing the sublime with the ridiculeous. Society seems to be making up for centuries of straight-jacket conformity imposed on everybody. Free Press is there to expose any irritant and bureaucratic ineptitude. What kind of religious belief he would have. He is not tied to the apron-strings of the grandparents for his keep. The neighbours are busy in their own affairs and do not go about bewailing the transgressions of others. Will he worship the family deity or chalk out his own routine including hedonist disbelief and vote for night life compared to the morning prayer, etc., a routine established in India from time immemorial. In any case what would one expect these days to ensue because of one's worship or daily prayer.

Tradition does not die easily. It only gets somewhat modified and stalk in another garb. No one has yet been able to shake the belief expressed in the *Gita* that one is free to work for his own good, but the results, profit or loss of his actions, lies in the hand of the gods or as ordained by fate. Modern man will thus not give up the traditional or new efforts to influence fate which include worship and prayer. He will not, however, believe any more in worship and prayer by proxy or through intermediaries. Priests will have less significance but the temples and altars where he can swiftly mark his presence will flourish. The superstitious hold of astrology will continue till benevolent robots can look after his welfare. Modern man will not any more trust magic or such activity to influence his fate. He will have an understanding of the benefits of silent group prayers or group songs in support of his beliefs and values.

Modern man will accept that the world is not strictly causal and, therefore, it is no longer necessary logically to accept re-birth or an after-life. One's actions may, however, leave an impression on his mind for future good or evil (in this very life) almost in the manner of *sanskara* of the Buddhists. Even if Einstein under the influence of his traditional learning said that God cannot be playing dice, one must accept that laws of probability rule the universe since that happens to be the nature of the most elementary particles that basically constitute the universe. Probabilistic behaviour really hints unfathomed complexity of present day ultimate particles. This is practically the teaching of the Jains, which has been in existence since the Vedic times and has many followers in India. Modern interpretation of the qualities of the most High is quite acceptable to him as he spontaneously is attracted to bliss, truth and consciousness. He will take part in social, religious rites and activities to the extent that pleases him and not for duty or for appearances. For respecting his own identity and that of his kinship group, he will continue to belong to traditional chapters of religion or politics. With the Protestants and Sikhs, he believes that the highest form of moral obligation is to fulfil one's duty in worldly affairs.

One can notice from the behaviour patterns of Indians who live abroad and have made it good in the USA, the U.K. or Canada that the more modern be their lives, the more devoted they are to traditional ways and to *satsang* and group prayers. We are certain that their faith is only pragmatic to bolster their self-image. They do not place their success at the door of the Lord. Only they believe that the prayer and worship might fend off adverse fate, and if these bring them more success, let them. Belief and disbelief leave their imprint on one's mind so that reward or retribution overtake it causally modified by the element of chance.

Modern man also will understand that mind has great potential, greater than one is aware of. To develop one's mind man uses traditional practices of *Yoga*, mental control, meditation, etc., but will question the trappings of fasting, celibacy, repetition of the Lord's name, etc. He will, however, accept the social necessity of an acceptable moral life. For such a modern man fanaticism will be anathema, but he will regard himself capable of any sacrifice for his own values. He will accept divinity in the religious belief of others and his own beliefs will have a multitude of gods and goddesses at various levels of his consciousness. Being free, he will find it hard to hand over his decision-making to a *guru*, priest or some symbol, but he will have respect for a person who lays down his life for the preservation of values esteemed by others as was done by Guru Teg Bahadur. He will not be a unit in a herd, but will like to exercise his wits in order to discriminate between various options.

Pursuit of Happiness

Ayn Rand has summarized the thinking of neo-radicals as favouring capitalism. She has been prophetic as we see the giant Communist States extolling the benefits of private enterprise for more production and less bureaucracy. Man must co-operate willingly and not through compulsion or from a sense of sacrifice or duty. The communes in China are breaking up and so did the experimental communes of the Mahatma. The joint family that has seen India through scarcity and travail is breaking up when the modern man has new opportunities for acquiring skills. Modern man will discover new values based on equality and freedom. Continuous and systematic work in a worldly calling would be the new asceticism. This was also preached and practised by Guru Nanak. Modern religion will include in its values industriousness and frugality. The historical relationship between religion and society or the traditional values cannot be brushed aside.

Modern scientific and religious values are reflected in the ten-point Gandhi-Gorbachov declaration (1986) of New Delhi. Peaceful co-existence must become the universal norm of international relations. Human life must be recognized as supreme. Non-violence (*Ahimsa*) should be the basis of community life. Understanding and trust must replace fear and suspicion. The right of every State to political and economic independence must be recognized and respected. Conditions must be generated for the individual's harmonious development. Resources being spent on armaments must be channelled towards social and economic development. Mankind's material and intellectual potential must be used to solve global problems. The balance of terror must give way to comprehensive international security. Nuclear weapons free and non-violent world requires specific and immediate action for disarmament.

One of the most important pre-occupations of the modern man will be to maximize his happiness. Ancient values exhort man to pursue economic well-being so that he can perform his family and social duties better and that he has leisure to pursue his salvation in his later life at least. Modern man will pursue riches for the sake of his happiness. He will be lucky if he remembers that the short-cut to one's happiness is to spread happiness to others. Modern man will like to be an achiever and win public acclaim. In order to achieve top standards, the chosen vocation must be demanding and absorbing. He will grasp the secret of true happiness that fair means and fair ends must be chosen. Modern man in the culture of work and of plenty will not be carried away by the evil counsel that sin or crime is there only if one is caught and will recognize the shaky foundations of success of smugglers and wind-bag politicians. There is always some hidden creative ability in all of us. Modern man will try to recognize his own aptitudes and talents. For creative contribution, one is to reach the limits of knowledge in a restricted field and then work hard with a will to succeed as the devotees of the Lord of old. Beyond worldly happiness beckons the contemplation of reality that is a reservoir of bliss.

9

DEMOCRACY

Introduction

DEMOCRACY MEANS a society where the citizens treat each other as equals. In a democratically-run polity there is freedom of speech, religion, opinion or association, and all adults have the voting right for electing representatives, a majority of whom then governs. For a moral society, there can be no substitute for democracy. The conventions for the formation of the government from out of the elected representatives and the way they give laws and appoint various authorities may, however, be different in different democracies. The world wars have also shown that democracies can succeed in the long haul when pitted against dictators.

Traditionally India has only idealized benevolent kingship responsive to advice of ministers selected by the rulers chiefly on merit and generally honouring traditional practices including differential treatment of various strata of society and groups. This was more like the controlled democracy experimented in Nepal recently. The king was traditionally expected to engage in public welfare. It was due to such traditions that the emperor Harshvardhan would give away every few years in charity the entire State treasure and start over again the husbanding of the State's resources. Punishments of the corrupt and unjust were severe and the king had his own spies and judges where necessary. Public works were diligently looked after. Ancient forts, temples, tanks, etc., are still standing and some are still in the original use. Populace was to follow religious and worldly duties under the watchful eyes of the elders, the king and the gods.

India usually had a bunch of kingdoms, though now and then a central authority would develop making most others as tribute-paying vassals. All the separate kingdoms tried to expand and people were used to feudal campaigns each year but the village life was not unduly disturbed and the village *panchayat raj* or local system of distributed authority continued in its placid stability. India continued to be ruled by such princes right up to the advent of British commercial power with a mercenary army. The position in the 18th and 19th centuries was chaotic. The country had become the hunting ground for all kinds of adventures with the weakening of the central rule and internecine warfare was intensified by the induction of foreign interests and mercenary forces.

The British also started as adventurers in the pay of different princes but their sense of national priority and indifference in their arrogance to moral norms when dealing with the natives helped them perfect the strategy of fanning strife to their advantage and they luckily succeeded in winning the control of whole of India. Hindus and Muslims were slowly developing regard for each other's holy men and developing a composite life. Many distinct castes were co-operatively functioning within the Hindu society and Hindus had philosophical acceptance of different gods and modes of worship. Hindu-Muslim understanding had reached a peak during the 1857 Mutiny which brought home to the colonists the value of the well-tried policy of 'divide and rule' of earlier empires of the Greeks and the Romans. Assiduously, in the name of non-interference in Indian religions, the fanatics of each community were encouraged to feel threatened by the other community.

The saner elements and the secular elements naturally had no love for the British and were suppressed in the name of security and the defence of the empire. Only such reformers whether Hindu or Muslim flourished who sided with the British ways or found fault with the other community more than with the foreigners. To the British from their experience of religious conflicts in Europe, India was a ready arena for Hindu-Muslim conflict which they fanned to the best of their ability and when more Indians joined the freedom movement, even Sikhs in the Punjab, non-Brahmins in Madras and Scheduled Castes everywhere were sought to be alienated from the Indian mainstream in spite of the obvious commitment to democracy and human rights from the nationalists, a great many of whom were Hindus by faith and were led by Mahatma Gandhi who was revered by the Hindus as *Mahatma*, a title usually reserved for religious divines among the Hindus. The British exercised arbitrary authority in India responsible only to the British Parliament. The British rule, however, was considerably mellowed by the efficiency and fair play by many individual British administrators who many times worked at cross purposes to colonial exploitation and wished to manage to the best of their ability in the way of bureaucracy primarily chosen on merit along with loyalty to the employer.

Many Europeans contributed to the introduction of modern science and technology in the country along with the methods of modern management. With the development of democracy in Great Britain, a shadow of democratic institutions was cast in the country but bedevilled with separate electorates, thus creating a permanent divide. Such a permanent divide is still persisting in the separate employment opportunities for certain suppressed classes of the past. The princes were kept propped up as an extra wheel of the empire who were trotted out as Indian leaders supporting the British power in international conflicts. Most Indian nationalists had advocated introduction of adult suffrage and unadulterated democracy on Independence.

Variety in Democracy

After the Western democracies won the two world wars, and as culmination of European political philosophy, 'democracy' was the in-thing for any political organization. So much so that even negations of democracy were labelled by the executioners of democracy as 'democratic regimes". Now an Islamic democracy stands for rule by a political party composed only of Muslims and obeying the *Koran* and the practice of the Prophet's rule during his campaigning in the seventh century Arabia as ultimate authority and precedent. Such a rule may somehow become acceptable to the dumb driven Muslim, but can never be an authentic democracy since so many non-conformists and non-Muslims are denied a say in the affairs of the land. Even majority rule can be irksome and undemocratic for the minorities. It is a convention that in a democracy the national interest would be supreme along with the human interest and strictly communal interest would not be imposed on others. In a feudal society where tradition holds away, the castes and guilds fully control the training and employment of the member families and everyone is the custodian of the pillory for the neighbour's behaviour. Primitive democracy in the form of *Panchayat Raj* functioned in the villages where each group allowed its elder to combine with other elders to run the limited functioning of the village government, viz. collection of king's taxes, local security, upkeep of tanks and temples and settlement of disputes referred to the *Panchayat* by anyone. It is said that the lasting quality of India's identity rests in the invention of the *Panchayat Raj*. This suited, as we said, a feudal State with limited communications and a completely decentralized economy and village-level self-sufficiency. When Nepal tried this system in the present times, it could only be a temporary respite from the incessant demand for modern amenities, since a *Panchayat Raj* of illiterate elders would only be arch conservative, though decentralization of authority would increase efficiency. Nepal has again opted for parliamentary democracy and is keen for friendship with the Indian democracy.

Single-party democracies are also in existence, for example, in the Soviet Union or Egypt. The Soviet system also frankly called itself a dictatorship of the proletariat, i.e. of the ruling Communist Party. But they are dismantling the system slowly but surely. Now they wish to introduce restructuring and openness in the country as well as in the party. Openness in the party means freer discussions and genuine attempts to form consensus on any issue and to carry the opposition within the party along. It is quite possible that for countries without the traditions for inter-party politics and the British way of conventions based on commonsense and public interest, the system of one-party government with assured internal party democracy and full scope for all to contend for arriving at a party consensus may be more appropriate. After all in an ideal multi-party democracy too each decision must carry the tacit forbearance of the opposition if not concurrence. A government has got to work for everyone's legitimate interests. In our own multi-party democracy, all parties play the game with no holds barred. Even after 40 years of independence trust is not placed in mutual promises and temporary nature of various problems requiring sometimes ad hoc measures in the national interest. They must be extra-methodical and amend the Constitution right and left. The opposition every now and then takes it into its head to stage a walk-out, hold a noisy demonstration in Parliament or takes to violent or non-violent protest marches outside. It appears we want to run the country after justifying ourselves to the bureaucracy or to win votes by *tamasha* rather than the well-known conservative or revolutionary programmes. I suppose with the slow pace in India, multi-party democracy will start working as it was meant to be in another 50 years or so. We have only now haltingly begun to use inter-party parliamentary committees to work on controversial issues for evolving agreed comprehensive legislation on any subject. Presently the question of election reform is on the anvil. The inter-party method has been well tried in the USA.

Just as dictators are trying to dismantle the dictatorial devices, the democratic rulers in certain countries are dismantling democratic institutions and handing over everything to single individuals calling them President and not dictator in a presidential form of government as in the USA. In USA the best insurance in favour of multi-party democracy is because of two almost equally balanced parties, but in most other countries, advocating the presidential form, it will only amount to the cult of personality or of a single party trampling on all opposition as in a dictatorship. India just scraped through escaping the presidential dead-end during Mrs. Indira Gandhi's regime. For the presidential form to succeed, there must be a free and fearless judiciary and considerable talent outside the bureaucracy and the armed forces. The Soviets are now opting for the presidential form since the head of the government now desires to have more freedom from the party bureaucracy and perhaps more control over the secret service.

Bicameral legislators are useful for large and federating countries. The upper houses provide a special channel to reach the classes not always represented properly by the masses of the voters. Perhaps the election reforms can invent ways to make the Lower House truly representative of the voters including essential interests of the nation and then the upper houses may become redundant. The Upper House can be misused by a minority government aware of its fagging popularity. The nominated representatives of special nation-building interests even when not in large numbers could make more impact in the Lower House itself.

Democracy in India

Under the Indian Constitution, the government in India is elected by the legislators. The Constitution assures fundamental rights to all and also legal equality irrespective of religion, region or caste. Broadly, the Indian democracy is as per the textbooks. In principle leaders of all revolutions have a high hope from the revolution, but usually the hopes go sour with time. In order to last, a revolution must be continuously watched and corrected with an ear to the feed-back from the public. One step backwards and two steps forwards is not an empty adage. It demonstrates willingness to take back any step in the interest of future progress. So long as they hold fast to the precious values, rest must be only tactics for success preferably consistent with morality. A democratic government must see to the interest of the common man and not just the interest of the ruling individuals or the ruling classes. The ruling elite alone has an interest in continued use of the English language and the government can hardly change this anomalous situation.

In a peaceful revolution that succeeded in India vis-a-vis the empire, there could be no suppression of reaction. On the partition of India too many immediate problems arose on account of the parting kick and immediate steps to proceed with economic equality could not be taken. The revolution stayed in the rare atmosphere of rhetoric and pious pronouncements in the form of egalitarian laws, but the political machinery was not there to see these implemented. Thus, we are still beset with mass killings of untouchables and tribals and a police force which is often a law unto itself. Charges of corruption and subversion of norms of democratic behaviour are rampant. If by some quirk of fortune, Netaji's armed movement had succeeded, one can imagine, casteism and communalism would have received short shrift. On the other hand one never knows as certain diseases, if suppressed too suddenly, have worst relapses as seems to be happening in neighbouring Bangladesh. The victory of secularism under the banner of Mujib proved a chimera and the country quietly passed into a dictatorship.

Though the separate electorates were abolished, yet the political parties remained very much conscious of the religious label of the electorate or of the candidates put up for election. Vote banks stayed in the pockets of caste elders and religion pushers. Even the feudal predilection of the elite and the subservience of the folks to the princes, the traditional symbols of pomp and power, continued. The non-communal political parties had to resort to communal calculations for winning elections. In addition to having been involved in the political struggle against the British and in the Mahatma's constructive work, considerations of financial resources, acceptance by religious power groups, even feudal hold on society, etc., were paramount for the grant of party tickets. After the lapse of few decades, with the diminishing memory of feudal lords and masters, and depletion by death and old age of the Congress stalwarts of the freedom struggle, now the accent is only on the loyalty to the political party or more correctly to the self-appointed supremo of that party and the fund-raising ability, the rest is left to the party image builders, modern means of mass communication, public relation experts and current heroes in the public eye like actors, sportsmen, journalists or reformed "notorious characters, etc." Prominent bureaucrats, wives and heirs of deceased politicians and some genuine persons engaged in the service of the people are also selected as candidates. True democracy should also lay down some criteria for selection of political party candidates, and we are certain many of the present-day criteria will not pass muster. In case the expected election reform can somehow permit a candidate to fight successfully an election on a shoe-string budget for a party not rolling in resources, the proper criterion can be made to stick. In the democratic system, the majority and the minority should mean political majority and political minority.

The policies endorsed by the majority must prevail and the minority can oppose such policies but within the rules of the democratic system, i.e. build up public opinion to defeat the current majority at the time of the next elections which are after all never far off. In India, however, we still have a hangover of communal majority and minority and the framers of the Constitution have laid down that no rule or law will be passed affecting any particular religious community without consulting the spokesmen of the community. The legislature must be having many members from the affected community, but they are silently downgraded from being spokesmen of the religious community since they have been elected via a political party. It was on this score that even a court endorsement of the politically sound decision in support of Muslim divorced women was overlooked and a conservative measure passed in consultation with self-proclaimed religious spokesmen. Perhaps this was good political insurance since in an old stagnant society sudden modernization can lead to violent reaction as had happened in neighbouring Iran or Afghanistan. But it was a wrong precedent to go over the heads of Muslim MPs to outside spokesmen of the Muslims. Even a conservative measure should have been stage-managed through the elected representatives in Parliament who were also Muslims. The convention and tradition of the supremacy of Parliament must be maintained so that communal centres of power are not endowed with political clout. Since we do wish to bring about modern thinking and advanced social measures, there is urgent need for sustained mass contact even at the religious level, and nationalists and secularists must infiltrate religious bodies in their religious role in the interest of national development. Maulana Azad was a nationalist to the core and was quite effective in religious pronouncements and organizations.

There are millions of secularist and nationalist Sikhs, Christians and Muslims who should not allow religious organizations in the clutches of reactionaries to continue to sow discord and thus weaken the nation. One is heartened by the political action of the Congress in Rajasthan on the question of temple entry of Harijans and Adivasis. Such a live issue should not have been left to Arya Samajists who are only a sectarian body though with nationalist instincts. We feel that the ruling party must pursue national goals more vigorously even outside the legislatures.

We should abolish reservation in different levels of government appointments. If the equal opportunities and economic average well-being is there, the proportions will naturally work out right. Apart from going all out to help the scheduled castes and scheduled tribes to amass educational and conversational qualities by means of liberal educational scholarship, subsidized camps or intensive coaching, there should not be any unmerited admissions and promotions. Like other successful rulers of this country or elsewhere, our government and employers must develop unbiased methods to locate merit and encourage and employ it. It is most ridiculous that the universities recognize sometimes merit and award merit scholarships, but the amount is usually not paid to the brilliant kid on the plea that he or she comes from a well-to-do family. Merit scholarships should be distinct from merit-cum-means stipends and should be treated as such for the encouragement and development of talent. In our free society, the success is measured by financial gain in general and no one else is limited by what one possesses except the merit grade students. The graded income-tax alone or the community levies can do the ironing out of wealth differences.

Conflicts and Elections

Democracy seeks to channel conflicts into electioneering, so that the country continues to function and develop under generally peaceful conditions albeit the policies not necessarily acquiesced in by the minority party will prevail under the Damocles' sword of possible change of government at the time of next elections. The minority is not supposed to take to extra-constitutional means to impose its own policies but conventions are sought to be made to blunt any violent disagreement by the minority when the measure is considered by the legislature. The process of election is thus a struggle between opposed views and majority vote will elect the representative who will represent the whole constituency for a brief period in the law-making and enforcing organization. Local issues and contending ideologies that might be exercising the electorate get thoroughly aired. If the elections are held in a fair way the struggles are temporarily suspended till the next election and the elected representatives run the government following the policies dear to the majority of the people. If the opposition is substantial in the legislature, naturally, in the interest of future success in the elections, the majority will not bull-doze any controversial legislation but seek consensus.

Practically, however, things are not so straightforward. Elections are fought with no holds barred. Personal as well as party failings are broadcast by the opponents. For swaying the election and influencing people, a lot of money is spent particularly when neither ever bothered to nurse the constituency. Generally, money power wins, the way the elections are held these days. There are now commercially available poll strategists and opinion moulders journalists and the media will discover many favourable things and advertise them for a fee. TV and radio time is also on sale. The first hurdle is to be selected as a candidate by a party more popular than the other parties. Normally the party should favour tried and trusted members of considerable standing, but the norms are not valid at the election time. They select on the basis of the expected ease of winning and then by the expected loyalty to the supremo, since our parties are invariably organized downwards from the top and are rarely grown from the base of ordinary members.

Violence in elections, booth-capturing, rigging, etc., are new maladies now occurring. A rigging of elections by the party in power and the unfair practices like bullying of election officers or voters or impersonation usually by activists of pessimistic parties are the signs that certain segments look at elections as a way to gain power somehow in alliance with the criminal elements. Communal or religious fanatics can also go to any length to vitiate elections in their own favour. Vigilant control by the authorities over fascist-type cadres has to be kept. The communalist cadres were particularly active in the democratic election victory of the non-Congress opposition – Janata party conglomerate. Most of the communal appeal is generated by parties and persons for winning elections. A substantial minority, if they plan ahead, can hijack the elections by winning 25 to 30 per cent of the total votes, especially if their candidate is opposed by more than one candidate and the average expected turnover of about 60 per cent happens at the time of voting. Thus a national party has to be particularly active in attracting voters from all walks whether political or religious or professional. The Akalis in the Punjab had less chance of forming a government because they used to go out of their way to alienate the substantial religious minority in the Punjab. The common man has to be watchful and must take part in elections en masse so that the turnover of more than 80 per cent eliminates chances of a hijacked election. More than a couple of popular candidates in the field also spoil the chance of a desired victory.

Already the voters in India are showing maturity and the parties no longer trust the old existence of vote banks. The voters are no longer voting as instructed by caste or feudal elders. In general they are showing their own class preference for the political parties, but they are stumped if the political party of their choice happens to give the ticket in its over-confidence to a non-entity or a lame horse. The voters are the consumers of the advertised stuff, i.e. the candidates seeking their vote. Just like the consumer movement, would it not be right for the voters to have guidance from non-party professionals regarding the personal merits of the candidates? This will also place the parties and their nominating committees on alert to put up candidates who have some contact with the local problems and the country's affairs, besides having genuine record of service and efficiency in whatever they have been doing. A non-party expert group could be put together in each constituency to explain their method of rating and then issue merit rating to the Press and radio for all candidates in the field, taking care not to involve any rating out of bias for the political party of the concerned candidate. The candidate evaluation should be truly based on the abilities and the record of his previous successes and efforts. The voter would then jettison any candidate of the party of his normal choice for a really superior person who would act fairly in the legislature and not blindly support or oppose measures. The conscience vote should be the norm rather than obedience to the party whip. In short, the voter wants his own and the national interest to be served by his candidate. (One can always expect the conscience of the candidate to be dyed in the party colour.) Even the political parties must have their own expert evaluation of the aspirants before they give anyone the nomination.

Religious, linguistic and elitist minorities can be influential, but their performance may not be in the national interest. The best antidote is to play down religion and charisma. Political debate should be on a national plane. Boycott of elections must be construed as an admission of defeat and the matter must go for a judicial as also the election process. There should also be a provision for the redressal, if possible, of the grievance of the frustrated group.

Majority and Minority

In India, whenever there is talk of a majority or minority in any electoral district, it is about religious majority or minority, a hang-over from the separate electorate days, or of majority caste and minority caste, etc. Such a division could continue to be permanent and the purpose of repeated elections and conversion of majority today to minority tomorrow or *vice versa* can be lost. A religious minority could hijack the government as discussed earlier in special circumstances or could bring the government to a standstill by aggressive disturbances and eventually lose much more than it might already have. Since the political rulers need not give rulings on religious problems, there is no case for fighting elections on religious labels. The majority and minority should be in terms of political philosophies. The obvious polarization can be in terms of traditionalism or conservation and pro-changers or the automation party. Most democracies settle down to such polarization. Many minor parties of various hues also exist but these do not count and if there are somehow more than a couple of equally popular parties, then the position becomes ripe for subversion of democracy by the active involvement of vested interests like the army or the bureaucracy or the foreign hand. In India we still lack a viable national opposition to the Congress Party which continues to mean different things to different people. It has all shades of philosophies though maximum lip service is paid to secularism and socialism. Already the Congress has split a few times after Nehru. When a split occurs on ideology, at that time we might expect a nucleus of opposition to begin. At the moment the opposition is on the basis of self versus the supremo. When both sides swear by Gandhi and Nehru, the opposition seems meaningless. One expects the Congress to grow more revolutionary and the opposition to settle for traditionalism. Ways must at once be found to curb multi-polar elections by special efforts to educate the voter not to vote for an independent, howsoever exalted he or she may be. This can be assured only if the independent rating of the party candidates is also consistently higher than that of the 'independents'. All those splinter groups whose candidates are certain to lose their security deposits should be offered a chance to bow out of the election at least a week before the election without prejudice to their security deposit. At the moment the Congress has the omnibus ideology of live and let live, provided one is loyal to an accepted political *guru* within the party and the opposition shows their zeal in claiming that they will make a better 'Congress' party since they have the genuine omnibus of all shades of values from right chauvinists to the left ones.

Given a secure world under the watchful eye of the strong United Nations of the future, do we favour surrounding our people with all kinds of gadgets and machines, computers and access to unlimited information and lonely bliss symbolized by automation or do we favour traditional religious and cultural pre-occupations, communal enjoyment of riches along with simple life and anti-consumerism for meeting necessities for the individual symbolized by the *charkha?* Thus, one may visualize the polarization of Indian polity. Our problem for quite some time will remain that our people will continue to kowtow to charisma. Perhaps the desired polarization awaits two distinct charismatic leaders of the two proposed ideologies. Thanks to planning and application of science, technology and modern management, the economics of scarcity will recede and the main problem will be of the pace of development and the choice of goals of scientific and technological progress.

Selection of Rulers

A structure of authority must exist to support and enforce conventions, taboos, rules and laws. The rulers constitute the pinnacle of such an edifice. In any society there are always certain important drives, e.g. education, philosophy, trade, production, emigration or colonization, tourism, etc., which require careful planning and promotion and the rulers must be enthusiastic for any such pre-occupations of society. In ancient times personal ability and experience were the only qualification. Age was, therefore, held in high esteem, and the advice of elders was a major element in ruling. Leadership bifurcated long ago in matters spiritual and temporal. In general in their mutual interest the two streams providing leadership co-operated and accepted traditionally assigned positions in the authority structure. When the temporal powers are expropriated by the chief priest in his own name or in the name of his god, the choice of such a ruler is made according to tradition using some superstition or some sacred descent.

When the progeny followed the trade of their forefathers, it was natural for the rulership to become hereditary. The oligarchs were less jealous of the princes of a royal household than someone from among themselves. The corrupting influence of power has always been present and one rarely meets a long line of effective kings. The corrupt or ineffective kings were overthrown by internal coups or external aggression. When the hereditary king reigned but did not rule leaving all exercise of authority to the chief minister the system was found to be more stable and has given rise to the existence of elected presidents who are titular heads while an elected prime minister wields the real power and is responsible to the public. The public elects democratically such rulers, but universal adult franchise is quite recent. In ancient democracies, whether in India or in Greece, the electoral power was with an oligarchy, the great majority of people had no direct say in the matter. If people are not watchful, democracy can be subverted by fascist groups and dictators can start functioning who by clever slogan-mongering may succeed in creating mass support for themselves suppressing all opposition. Leftist dictatorships do no less, but they often replace worse regimes. The ballot monitors the disaffection and makes it legitimate.

On the British pattern of democracy applicable in our country the government is formed by the majority party of the legislature which then selects the prime minister who picks up his team of ministers from among the members of the legislature. If he needs someone from outside the legislature, the newly inducted person has to get elected to the Lower or the Upper House within six months. The public stays supreme by usually balancing two parties pretty much evenly so that they can always oust the unsatisfactory performer at the next elections. The voting and elections on party lines helps in the stability of the ruling team especially when defection from the party that got him elected is frowned upon and can cancel one's election.

We have yet to build new conventions within the party as well as within the legislature so that we can avoid dissidence, corruption, flattery and violence. There should be no place in free India, with assured democratic rights of citizens and an efficient law enforcement, for persecution or violence. When we see violent regional agitations ending in sensible agreements, it should become quite clear that something has been wrong in the rulers remaining ignorant of the real problems of the people in those areas. But if a terrorist group has no popular base or public interest at heart and whose only aim is to usurp power after murdering popular leaders who stand up to them, then there is no alternative but to suppress them firmly. Civil wars have been fought for much less. In democracy the minority parties should form responsible opposition and allow the majority to rule for its allotted term and not obstruct the government's functioning by all kinds of agitations, *bandhs* and orchestrated violence. Could not we build new ways to oblige the opposition to become responsible? In mathematical terms healthy correlation is admitted only if the majority party is more than 66 per cent. We should limit the term of party in power proportional to its true representative character. If its majority in the electoral college (Lower House) is 66 per cent or more it should govern for the full term till the due date of next elections. But if its strength is less, it must vacate the governance somewhat earlier and for the remaining period till the next elections, there should be President's rule with bipartisan advisers or advisers at least one each from all parties with at least, say, 10 per cent of the strength of the electoral college. This will give the opposition parties a stake in stable government and also some feel of the actual working of the government and the usual single-point programme of displacing the prime minister will cease since he is going to step down any way near the elections. Similar practice can be included in selecting party leaders so that the preoccupation of ambitious people towards displacing the elected chief becomes meaningless, since all contending party leaders can share the period of power allotted to the majority party.

There is still the larger question of fitness of candidates set up for election and to rule. At present for the important job of becoming a ruler, there is neither any training nor any test. The candidates should perhaps be picked up for their distinction in some walk of life, for their deep study and insight, lucid expression and willingness to lead as well as to work in a team. We have already entered the technological age. Will our rulers understand the impact of technologies as they emerge on the Indian scene. Some of our current rulers have personal history rather wanting in principle or in constructive work. Political parties may do well to start choosing and developing potential rulers by making them understudies to effective leaders in industry, politics, information, new technologies, etc. The selection must not continue on the basis of flag waiving and sycophantic behaviour. They have to demonstrate their commitment to planned development, hard work, constructive service and honesty in word and deed. They have to be committed to the values of secularism, freedom from prejudice and superstition.

10

COMBATING CONFLICTS

Introduction

MAN HAS thousands, of, years of experience of continuous conflicts and only now there is some glimmer of hope that the world may have approached the beginning of the end of conflicts. Half the battle is won if one were to foresee an approaching conflict situation and plan in advance to forestall it and be adequately ready to resolve and sublimate the conflict situation. The policy-makers have to keep their balance and not rock the boat of history by leaning too much on either side of any issue. Parties to any conflict must learn from all kinds of precedents to welcome peace-making and negotiate a synthesis of the temporarily opposing views. Parties to a possible conflict may learn from the lessons of history the disadvantage in prolonging any conflict and the benefit in seeking its resolution through peaceful talks. Iran and Iraq have learnt this the hard way and India and Pakistan often forget what they have learnt at great cost. One in conflict often attaches, in a ridiculous way, the life-and-death importance to ones own position in the conflict. The world to him is wholy yea or nay. Such parties must realize that eventually the truth and the middle path will prevail. Most people among the followers of each side may be carried away temporarily by the Goebblian propaganda but in their heart of hearts, hope and love of peace lingers. The power that prevails rests with the silent majority of ordinary citizens intent on peaceful pursuits and with the environment including the world at large, which is much bigger than the well where the frogs might be at loggerheads. In the past even an earthquake in one valley hardly mattered to people in the next valley. With modern communications and an altruistic accent on international affairs of the present days of peace and plenty opposed to the affairs of olden times of struggle and scarcity, the whole world takes notice when peace is threatened anywhere, and the world is truly attempting to be a large family. Great responsibility, however, rests on the media, charismatic leaders and the youth.

Roots of Conflict

Primarily the roots of conflict lie in the exploitation or attempted exploitation. When the ancient civilizations were at their peak, no one bothered to see the seeds of future conflicts in slavery or untouchability. The Greek and the Roman civilizations were forgotten because of slave rebellions and the turn of the wheel of fortune. Eventually slavery was placed at a relatively higher pedestal by the Turks and slaves served them well in peace and war. To the extent the Hindus mistreated the outcastes and tribals, they lost their own freedom and when Hindus made changes in their value system within the living tradition and philosophy, their civilization revived phoenix-like. So many reformers and saints constantly preached equality of all men and all gods. Untouchability has been abolished as a culmination of an evolutionary process. Even the so-called break with tradition on account of many untouchables embracing Buddhism is hardly a revolution since most people regard Buddhism as a brilliant off-shoot of Hinduism.

Many eminent Indians realized in time the seeds of Hindu-Muslim discord sown by the British, but since the power was with the British, partition did take place but theoretically the partition was based on the democratic wishes of the population in contiguous areas in the east and the west of India. The communal riots and migrations were not part of the partition plan but entirely due to miscalculation of the communalists out to exploit religious minority or to expel it. The communal virus released in India in the first half of 20th century before partition is still not eradicated. Part of the disease has been transferred to mutual distrust between the sovereign nations of India and Pakistan, but part of it still bedevils communal or linguistic relations in certain regions of India and Pakistan. The students of Indian affairs must have noticed that in all-India politics affecting the government of the whole country from the centre, the authorities seem to be satisfied with the secular politics claimed by the Congress ruling at the Centre and the Janata Party when it ruled there. The all-India religious minority communal parties like the Muslim League, the Akali Dal etc., were quite willing to go along with them or make electoral pacts, but it is these very parties when operating in States that blame the national parties for communalism and discrimination. When an all-India minority happens to be the religious majority in the State in question, e.g. Sikhs in the Punjab or Muslims in Kashmir, the non-Hindu communal parties wish to swear with communalism so that they can perpetuate the rule of fanatics and exploit the religious minorities, but otherwise, since in the whole of India they cannot, being religious minority, ever hope to form a communal government they would like to encourage secularism. It is partly the duty of Sikhs outside the Punjab and Muslims outside Kashmir to see that their co-religionists everywhere eschew communal politics and encourage secularism throughout the land for internal peace and progress in the country. Since there are no longer the British overlords present in India to keep propping up communalism, soon secularism will triumph in all parts of the country. There has been suicidal opposition to secularism by certain Sikh students in Bidar or in Jammu where the Sikhs are in a microscopic minority.

The conflict of the generation gap is resolvable only through understanding and love from the elders. The climate of grabbing and intense competition is not conducive to the desirable qualities of sharing and co-operation. The value of private profit to be sublimated to altruism without the prop of religion or Marxism requires intense humanism and systematic thought about *Sarvodaya*, so dear to the Mahatma. Some of our misguided youth succumb to the pressure seen against the established values of justice and fair play, forgetting that thus they are inviting future disaster and anarchy. It is only when they often see among their elders examples galore of unmerited success through negation of cherished values and outright knavery, like crime and smuggling, that they lose heart about claims of morality. Insincerity and consumerism are on the ascendant at the moment.

India has already had a few occasions to measure its armed strength with that of Pakistan and with that of China. We have unresolved border problems with both these countries. We believe that whatever the British did not hand over to Pakistan belongs to India and thus the whole of J & K State, Aksai Chin plateau, Arunachal State are parts of India. On the other hand not only our neighbours have preferred claims against us but also have forcibly grabbed parts of Kashmir State and the whole of Aksai Chin and continue to do sabre-rattling across the glaciers of Kashmir and the mountain passes in Sikkim and Arunachal. At the moment the three countries hope to resolve the issues by negotiations while expecting all the time that the other side would climb down in the bargaining or lower its guard for a quick armed test. What should be the strategy for international peace and victory of truth? India-China problems regarding border areas are also connected to the autonomy of Tibet for which the people of Tibet are struggling though many Chinese have now been forcibly settled there. The Tibetan problem might escalate like the Palestinian problem in not too distant a future. India-Pakistan policies are also clouded by the terrorist activities in Punjab and Kashmir and the opposition of the Pushtuns for vassalage of their homelands in Pakistan, which might again blow up when the position in Afghanistan crystallizes with a nationalist secular regime there. In the area from the Indian borders to the Russian borders across Pakistan and Afghanistan, the non-Muslim religious minorities have fallen from about 20 per cent to one per cent in the last century. During and before Ranjit Singh's time many influential civil appointments in all this area were based on merit and were often held by non-Muslims. Now the few Hindus and Sikhs are engaged only in trade and commerce. Just as the Russians have been willing to make peace in Afghanistan provided there is a non-aligned government in Afghanistan, our minimum requirement would be for a secular State in Pakistan and in Afghanistan, which meets with the aims of the founding fathers of Pakistan as well as the aims of the people in Afghanistan. Most likely the border problems with Pakistan will be only of anti-terrorism and anti-smuggling and not of territorial jurisdiction. With a non-expansionist China or an autonomous Tibet, our border can be a border of friendship and not border of division. The three countries must think now how to sort out these border issues so that no festering sores are left for the future generations.

Fanaticism and schismatic beliefs today give rise to future conflicts. We must do everything to familiarize our people with the piety and beliefs of other faiths. All group worship must be open to all worshipful individuals to whatever persuasion they may belong and there should be no bar for worshippers not sporting sectarian symbols or slogans. It should be common knowledge how to worship in different ways commonly met in the country. Radio and television can play some part in it through the good offices of the Integration Councils already functioning. Co-existence of various beliefs in society or in the same individual must be widely accepted.

Principle of Synthesis

Philosophers claim that most propositions have a negation too. Advancement occurs when there is a synthesis at a higher plane of formulation. Vegetarianism and non-vegetarianism often compromise on certain diet preferable to both the types. Certain professed vegetarians take eggs or fish. Capitalism and socialism have shown remarkable co-existence in our own socialistic pattern of society. Neo-capitalists believe in efficiency of private profit but not in the exploitation of the unwary. Mahatma Gandhi's theory of trusteeship was almost neo-capitalist. Anand Margis and the Khalistani terrorists insist that the only persons fit to rule were their own comrades. Their views could be assimilated by the public by democratic vote for idealists rather than for the *Aya Rams* and *Gaya Rams*. The synthesis would be by locating idealists in all kinds of political parties and not simply in the company of Pol Potists or Naxalites, etc., terrorist groups.

The Sikh Gurus gave the best synthesis of existing religious philosophies and their teaching is valid for all time, in spite of the aberration by the Sikh communalists. The Punjabis were burying their heads in sand as an ostrich does, when the Singh Sabhas, under an agreement with the British, claimed to clean the gurdwaras of Hindu symbols and the Hindus of the vicinity attempted to build separate Hindu shrines in competition with the popular gurdwaras. Sikh Gurus were great Hindu heroes and worshipped Hindu gods and goddesses personally but in reformed ways. The best approach for synthesis now is again to worship in composite temples open to all, here we mean temples in which religious symbols dear to various religious people are placed cheek by jowl for worship and we are not referring to multi-religious places of meditation built by single groups, like the Baha's or the Ramakrishna Mission or a new fangled Japanese shrine for silent meditation before an empty cell, full of space and vacuum. Classical languages are very useful for access to ancient wisdom towards progress of thought, but our daily prayer must not be confined to the little understood ancient languages; the common man should be enabled to perceive the potency of prayer in a group when he understands what he is asking for.

Can the Muslim League and the PPP in Pakistan achieve a synthesis or can the Jan Morcha and the Congress do so in India? They certainly can, as most of the actors are chips of the same block. A simple synthesis is by accepting the logic of democracy and sharing power by healthy conventions of taking major decisions by consensus and giving further play to inter-party committees or at least agreeing peacefully to share power in tandem or even in the same term under the proportional strength rule suggested earlier.

The current entrenchment of the English language in the country and premium being placed on knowledge of science and technology, including medicine through the knowledge of English, is going to be a source of extensive future conflicts between the haves and have-nots of English education. The verdict of English-knowing people of the West is that ordinary English education in India, barring that in a few large cities and of a few talented individuals, is horrible in grammar, pronunciation or spelling and the only thing they learn is the alphabet and writing their names in English. The new better salaried class of English-knowing people will soon become strangers in their own country. A violent nationalism is bound to upset the international pretensions of this class. A synthesis beckons in developing the Vishwa Karma language (like Urdu of the pre-British days) that of Hindustani with a smattering of English vocabulary particularly useful in sciences and using the phonetic Roman script which is no longer foreign to most Indians. Even many common English words are preferred to be spoken on TV and radio or by film heroes and heroines.

A Positive Approach

One must develop awareness of nascent conflicts and be prepared to meet them in advance. We must not try to sweep our current conflicts under the carpet or just whitewash and perfume the dirt or attempt outright to suppress them. In Zanzibar forced inter-racial marriages were performed. It is wrong to pretend absence of conflict in statements like Indian women are worshipped like goddesses or the Muslim women are better off or in Brazil there is no slavery, only the Negroes know their place, etc. When we are concerned with identifying future conflicts, the exhortation of seeing, hearing and speaking no evil does not work. A conflict will not be suppressed by outlawing it or declaring and imposing a single-party rule or a partyless democracy. We have examples of Burma and Pakistan before us. Basic values of truth, non-violence and co-existence can hope to alleviate conflict and re-channel it into pathways of synthesis. If any belief or action seeks to curtail the equal liberty of others, or create economic or ecological hazards for others such actions must be exposed and curbed firmly. If people are trusted to care for the security of the country, its Constitution and the rights of other citizens, privately-owned radio and television stations can become an asset for the integration in our view. On the other hand unbridled advertisements for consumerism only underscore the feelings of being left out and of unbearable injustice to the poor. A superior ploy would be to provide the advertised luxuries to co-operatives on hire-purchase basis so that the poor can also have the joy of sharing such luxuries. Many social organizations could assist tourism for the poor by arranging cheap group tours and pilgrimages. There can still be tremendous market in India if only co-operatives and public places, like the temples and *dharamsalas*, are enabled to become customers of high priced consumer equipments.

The positive approach to the elimination of conflicts must be that conflicts are handled at the level of controversies requiring discussions and resolution towards synthesis. People must understand that co-existence alone can make them tenants for the common home — that is India.

Counselling

Third party arbitration or at least the acceptance of a third party as counsellor to both sides for the purpose of resolution of conflict can be very useful once the conflict is out in the open and has resulted in confrontation or expected confrontation. This is possible only if at least some channel of trustworthy communication is kept open. The Gandhi-Irwin Pact came about because well-known Indian liberal politicians had the trust of both sides for communications. Family quarrels have shown the advantage of counsel from elders. Counselling must work also for social and political conflicts. But it has to be provided by professionals who are trusted to be impartial from professional sense of responsibility. The U.N. Secretary General played a very important role as counsellor and go-between for bringing about the resolution of major problems recently. The Israelites had taken over from the Nazis who were their oppressors in Europe, the practice of oppressing a minority and almost carried out genocide against the Palestinians making the remaining Palestinians, who could not flee to any other place, second-class citizens in their own country. This conflict is vitiating the atmosphere in the entire Middle East.

Now that Iran-Iraq conflict is over, the world attention will again be drawn to the festering sores – the Palestinian situation and the racial arrogance in South Africa. South Africa has also seen and understood the writing on the wall and given up its claims to rule Namibia and has set free Mandela, the symbol of Black South Africa's struggle for equality and democracy, in their own land usurped by European settlers who constitute a substantial minority. How long can they trust their luck to hold against the hostility of the entire world. This is the right time for South Africans both white and black to have more meaningful discussions how to dismantle apartheid and usher in democracy. The technology and the capital as well as the management skill of the white minority could be very useful to democratic South Africa and the white-controlled interests must no longer be interested in cheap illiterate labour through apartheid and oppression. Automation and technological advances now require educated and contented labour.

Even in the ancient past, the civilizations based on slave labour crumpled when a whiff of liberty was encountered from the soldiers of Rome or from the soldiers of Islam. The white South Africans living in peace and amity with the African blacks can take over the role of change agents for the entire continent of Africa. The wisdom seems to be dawning on the racialists especially when their chief supporter, the USA, is also convinced that just as it happened in the United States, where the blacks had to be integrated in the American society, in the same way there is no future for apartheid in South Africa or anywhere else. The South Africans and Angolans have already withdrawn from open conflict.

The gross distortion of Sikh history by the expatriate Sikhs in the U.K., Canada and the USA should bring home to India that she cannot afford to miss proper religious education of Indians settled abroad. It is the priests who have gone from India who carried the virus of communalism for them to intensify and send it back with financial resources to subvert democracy in the Punjab. Indian religious bodies should be encouraged to finance sending out able teachers of Indian religions abroad who can explain the difference between the dictatorial Delhi Durbar of Mughal days and the democratically elected and responsible Central government now functioning from Delhi and the vigorous democratic politics prevailing in the Punjab but for the nefarious activities of the foreign financed and trained terrorists. This can be a kind of preventive counselling for the future. India must apprise the world of the wisdom of the Buddha and of Gandhi and the choice of the middle path, of co-existence and secularism for the whole world. It is easy to see from history that most nations around India followed the path trodden by India in the past whether of Harappan civilization or Hindu-Buddhist teachings or Islamic culture. Now one after the other, most countries will take to non-alignment, new economic order secularism and co-existence. The present-day distortions in the minds of distant Indian communities or in Fiji are only an aftermath of recent Indian bondage and inertia in the people's minds. Most countries are bound to welcome Indian values since all of them hope to achieve unity in diversity. Democracy and co-existence among diverse elements go together.

Opinion Moulding

India is considered to be quite experienced in opinion moulding. This is primarily because of the stalwarts of the freedom struggle especially Mahatma Gandhi who had the knack to use media for influencing his own public as well as the public of Great Britain. Nehru almost single-handed welded the Third World into a working force for peace and progress in the world. Opinions in tune with the times spread very easily. Opinion moulding is a constructive approach and brain-washing is almost the same thing but serving the interests of some-one else and never those of the person being brain-washed. Similarly the misinformation techniques go against the genuine interests of the public. Opinion moulding has grown out of the war-time efforts of pro- and anti-propaganda indulged by both sides. Goebbles is considered to be the father of lies or misinformation. He has given the dictum that a lie repeated hundreds of times takes on the appearance of truth. After all many religious verieties have become established truths because these have been repeated thousands of times from all kinds of pulpits and from the mother to the child. Khalistan problem had arisen because of the captive Sikh audience in the Gurdwaras reciting praises every day of the sacrifices endured by true Sikhs at the hands of the Delhi rulers (centuries ago) and then quietly identifying the present Central government as the Delhi ruler of old. By a change of word or its connotation here and there in the true Machiavellian style, Bhindranwale completely distorted Sikh history and ethics.

Freedom can never be a licence. So long as there is no democratic and secular utopia in the country, the common man must be vigilant and refuse to accept any stone, hair, *yantra* or *mantra* as superior to the Indian Constitution that permits us all equality and freedom and allows our respective faiths to be practised and preached. The pulpit will never again be polluted with propaganda for hatred among fellow Indians. Pulpits on the other hand can support integrating activities like celebration of popular festivals even if they have affiliation with a particular religion, like Diwali, Id, Christmas, Baisakhi, Durga Pooja, Ganesh Chaturthi, Urs of famous saints, Holi, etc. The minority accent on separation and aloofness is counter-productive in a democracy with equality before law.

Advertisers understand the methodology of opinion moulding. The technique relies on a small element of truth or half truth clothed in voluminous amount of material of mostly unconnected truths and respected or loved material so that the desired message is associated with good reflections. Analogies, similarities of words, well-known rhythms, implications and associations are used. Exaggeration is avoided so far as the objective information is concerned but exaggeration about extraneous matters is in order. Children, beautiful ladies, gods and goddesses, heroes, babies, heroic moments in the memory of the public are all grist for the mill of the opinion moulder : propagandist or advertiser alike. The phrase 'Gandhi cap' was invented, for example, for moulding opinion in favour of the cap of *Khadi* for all. Most persons are swayed by different carrots and different sticks and so one uses all kinds of attractions for the desired message at the same time or at different times. Opinion moulding for birth control has collected a large repertoire of attractions for both the volunteer and the motivator.

The major task for the opinion moulders in our country is to make people truly more religious so that they realize the essential unity and peaceful ambitions of religion. We have radio and TV quizes for sports and science. It would be more important to hold quizes for religion asking Hindu competitors about Islam and Muslim competitors about Hinduism in the presence of knowledgeable authorities and also about historical instances of secularism and democracy. Respect for a religion must arise from its good points, piety of its votaries and sacrifices and courageous action of its pious men.

Radio, TV and films are a powerful medium for opinion moulding. Some self-supervision becomes obligatory. Radio and television should have paid viewers to critically appreciate the programmes and to provide correctives and feed-back in the interest of democracy and secularism in the country. Any programme even remotely spreading obscurantism and superstition must be curbed excepting the fairy tales for children and mythology for the senior citizens who understand the true worth of mythology. Myths should not be intermingled with modern themes and persons, since this spreads either obscurantism or disrespect for the faith of many people. The same holds for miracles. Well-repeated miracles in the holy books may be broadcast without derogatory or doubting comments, but an imaginary miracle befalling the common people due to a special or specific prayer or religious observance need not be shown since we may again only be spreading ignorance and short-cuts in place of hard work. The rendering of the *Ramayana* on TV has been done in a most successful and popular fashion, bringing the epic closer to many who were not very much familiar with it. Maybe other enterprising producers can do justice to the lore of other religions and cultures also.

Commercial advertisement must be reoriented in favour only of essentials, and for luxuries only for public places and co-operative living if consumerism has to be presented in low-key so long as we are not as rich as modern consumerism requires.

Idealist cinema and progressive writers do not make money. Only a popular newspaper can aspire to mould opinion in a substantial measure. For becoming popular, the newspaper must cater to many tastes and the editor has to be extra careful not to hurt the feelings of the owners, advertisers, government, local authority, etc. A journalist's life is not a bed of roses. Many depend on him to guide their views about happenings. He has got to be fearless when the occasion demands but he has also to be resourceful and slippery like an eel when collecting his news and putting it across.

The successful people, social and political figures who make news also mould public opinion by the statements they make and the lives they lead. Many people get their views from the published interviews with the film stars in a whole class of film magazines.

Modern Values

Values are very important since these censure the goals and the means adopted. Values constitute the conscience of a society. Just as an individual functioning against his conscience soon loses all self-respect, in the same way if the actions do not conform to the recognized values, the individuals will lose social recognition and internal and external conflict will start. Primarily values evolve form an ancient base, slowly changing their content and significance. Totally new values are also formed depending on quantum steps in human or environmental changes. A sudden reversal of values makes the common man feel insecure in the new world and feeling of security is essential for continued happiness. The glorification of violence, e.g. Mao's dictum that power flows from the barrel of a gun, proved to be a temporary slogan. Dr. L.B.M. Joseph has diagnosed that the technological advances have de-humanized relationships, i.e. the human culture. A new emphasis on group activities rather than solitary striving has to be enshrined in the modern value system. Ethical values of truth, honesty and sincerity are valid for all times while the competitive environment has created new values of aggressive leadership and self-interest which often go against the basic ethical values. Some values like respect for women and elders are losing their old reverence. Loyalty to the King was a supreme value in feudal times in Asia or Europe, but a new age of contempt for such institutions began with Mark Twain and George Bernard Shaw. At one time high education meant the knowledge of classical languages and classics, now it only means in India fluency in English.

There is convergence of ethical values and values cherished in scientific work, e.g. striving for truth, suspended judgement, exploration of new ideas, objectivity and honesty of means, etc. Male vanity and womanly subservience are giving way to comradeship and equality of sexes but there are pronounced generation-gap reactions.

The spread of democracy also means spread of art and culture to almost everybody. This is perhaps the key for understanding modern art which is folk art of the technological age. In the same way the new trends in music forms must be a result of generalization by the common man in place of specialization of the masters.

Conclusion

We have presented the detection and prevention of conflicts, going over their nature and ways of spreading. Declaration of a country as a State associated with a particular religion will not eradicate communalism. The human mind and its freedom and variety are such that such a step will only bring about suppression and rebellion. Fiji is playing a 'Christian' country by a declaration curbing the non-Christian — the late entrants — even though they constitute almost the majority of the population. A country even tries to ask a segment of its population to give up alien sounding names in favour of national integration. Any such compulsion for conformity is no solution but only an attempt at suppression of the possible conflict. The United States of America first attempted a genocide of the American Indians, then tried to herd them into reserves, but the technological and cultural developments have been such that now they are being given full citizen status and encouraged to prosper on their own.

Unity in diversity is the best goal for any nation or for the entire world. Each mind is complex and itself is a unity in diversity. Scientific approach, secularism and co-existence are the values that can guide people to happiness in the complex modern world. Social justice is the contribution of the materialist philosophy to world culture while secularism and humanistic approach is the contribution of ancient philosophies, both theist and atheist. Present-day thinking is approaching the same values by an objective examination of the universe.

God, the day of judgement, the certainty of rewards and punishments for deeds already done, religion and social rituals have an eternal hold on the people's minds essentially for their own good. Freedom not to conform may not be taken as unwanted aberration, but must be recognized as the natural way for evolutionary development. God appears differently to different minds and each one is welcome to its own conception. For a thickly populated country like India, unity in diversity and co-existence along with open discussions on new ideas are essential for growth and prosperity and for containing future conflicts.

GLOSSARY

Ahimsa	=	Non-violence
Akal Takht	=	Seat of the leader of a representative assembly of the Sikhs in Amritsar from which binding pronouncements are made for them
Atma	=	Soul
Aya Ram and Gaya Ram	=	A political defector, turncoat
B.A.R.C.	=	Bhabha Atomic Research Centre at Bombay
Bhakt	=	One engaged in *Bhakti*, i.e. devotion to the Lord
Bhrigu	=	Legendary astrologer who is supposed to have cast the horoscopes of the whole mankind for all times
Brahmand	=	According to Hindu mythology, the universe came out of the universal egg known as Brahmand
CPM	=	Critical Path Method for project planning
C.S.I.R.	=	Council of Scientific and Industrial Research in India
Charkha	=	Spinning wheel, a symbol of rejection of consumerism and large-scale factory production
Charuvak	=	Ancient Indian sage of pre-Vedic age who taught unadulterated materialism with no acknowledgement of soul or God
Chipko	=	A movement of environmentalists where non-violent protection of trees is attempted by embracing them, thus foiling the wielders of the axe

Dharma	=	Essential quality. Right conduct often translated as religion, Hinduism, or humanism
Dharamsala	=	A charitable guest house for pilgrims at nominal charge
ESP	=	Extra-sensory perception
Gita	=	Hindu holy book containing the essence of Dharma as taught by Lord Krisna to Arjuna at the outset of the Mahabharata war
Gorkhaland	=	Indian area around Darjeeling close to Nepal where there was no restriction for Nepali citizens to come and go and majority of the population is Indian Gorkhas of Nepalese origin
Gurdwara	=	A prayer hall with a shrine for the *Guru Granth Sahib*, the holy book of the Sikhs
I.P.K.F.	=	Indian Peace Keeping Force invited by Sri Lanka to disarm Tamil terrorists wanting free Tamil Eelam in Sri Lanka
Jainism	=	An Indian religion with an extra emphasis on *Ahimsa* and suspended judgement in philosophy
Jambu Dweep	=	The world Island of Hindu conception about twice the size of present India
Karma	=	Deeds that bear fruit in this or the next life
LTTE	=	Liberation Tigers of Tamil Eelam who are in revolt in Sri Lanka
Mahatma	=	Great Soul – A popular title of respect to a religious person and who can guide others.
Mukti, Moksha	=	Salvation; the soul is liberated from the cycle of re-birth
N.A.M.	=	Non-Aligned Movement of nations who do not join the major military pacts in opposition to each other
Nirankari	=	Worshippers of the formless. A modern sect which believes in the necessity of guidance by a living *guru*, besides the guidance from the *Guru Granth Sahib*, very popular among Sindhis and Punjabis.

PERT = Project Evaluation Research Technique very useful in planning

PPP = Pakistan People's Party

Panchayati Raj = Village self-government through elected village councils known as Panchayats in existence in India from hoary past, now being used as an instrument of de-centralization in an Indian version of perestroika.

Pir = A Muslim religious preceptor, a holy man, practically a *guru* to his followers among Hindus and Muslims alike

Qazi = A judge in an Islamic court

SAARC = South Asian Association for Regional Co-operation

Samadhi = A monument over the ashes or a funerary casket

Sangha = Buddhist organization of monks for the preservation and spread of Dharma

Samskara, Sanskara = The imprint of an individual's deeds on his soul according to the Hindus and on the 'web' of life, according to the Buddhists. Re-birth/*mukti* depend on the sanskara

Sanyasi = One who has given up worldly possessions and attachments

Sarvodaya = A philosophy of universal uplift associated with Mahatma Gandhi

Sati = An ideal Hindu wife who could contemplate immolating herself on the funeral pyre of her dead husband. The immolation act, however, is now illegal

Satsang = A gathering engaged in religions chanting or discourse

Sufi = Muslim divine who believes in divine love

Tamasha = A spectacle meant to entertain a crowd

Yoga = A physical and/or mental discipline for physical health and spiritual progress which can be practised by anyone especially *yogis*

BIBLIOGRAPHY

Abidi A.M.H., Islamic fundamentalism in West Asia. *Mainstream*, Vol.26, (23), p.25.

Bardis, Panos D. (1987). 'Jensenism and Inter-racial Peace', *Int. J. World Peace*, Vol.4, p.77.

Brandt, Wily (1980). *North-South*, M.I.T. Boston.

Dhirendranath (1940). *The Problem of Minorities*, University of Calcutta, Calcutta.

Dorsey, Larry, M.D. (1982). *Space, Time and Medicine*, Boulder and London, U.K.

Egner, Robert, E. (1975). *Bertrand Russell's Best*, Unwin Books, London.

Engineer, A. Ali (1988). Sufism and Communal Harmony, *Mainstream* (July 2), pp.19-23.

Enloe. Cynthia H. (1972). *Ethnic Conflict and Political Development*, Little Brown & Co. Boston.

Haider, Tariq (1985). *Indian Ocean – A Zone of Peace*, Secular House, New Delhi.

Hofstadter, D.R. and Daniel C. Dennet (1982). *The Mind's I*. Penguin, U.K.

Kothari, D.S. (1987). *Science and Ahimsa*, Delhi University, Delhi.

Lowenhard, Parcy (1987). The open society, Peace and Freedom Special Report, (PWPA) Professors World Peace Academy, Paragon-House, New York.

Mahmood, Syed (1949). *Hindu-Muslim Cultural Accord*, Vora & Co., Bombay.

Mayer, K.E. (1986). *Violence and Aggression*, Paragon House, New York.

Nanda, J.N. (1982). 'Election of Rulers', *Gandhi Marg*, 36, p.742.

Nanda, J.N. (1986). *Science & Technology in India's Transformation*, Concept Publishers, New Delhi.

Narain, Govind, (1986). *National Security Lectures*, U.S.I.S., New Delhi.

Piven, F.F. and R.A. Cloward, (1978). *Poor Peoples Movements*, Vintage Books, New York.

Rand, Ayn (1961). *For the New Intellectuals*, New American Library, New York.

Russell, Bertrand (1976). *A Free Man's Worship*, Unwin Paperbacks, London.

Sarawathi, S. (1974). *Minorities in Madras State*, Inpex India, Delhi.

Sattar, M. Abder (1947). *National State and National Minorities*, Lahore.

Sutherland, R.L. and J.L. Woodward (1940). *Introductory Sociology*, Lippen Cott Co., New York.

Thompson, Virginia and Richard Adoff (1935). *Minority Problems in South-East Asia*, Russel and Russell, New York.

Weber, Max. (1976). *The Protestant Ethic and the Spirit of Capitalism*, Allen and Unwin, London.

Whitaker, Ben (1972). *The Fourth World*. Schodress Brothers, New York.

Yetman, Norman, R. and C. Holystack (1975). *Majority and Minority*, Alyn and Bacon, Boston, USA.

INDEX